Millennium Dawn Publishing
Copyright 2011 © Robin Sweet-Ransom
Second Publishing 2014
ISBN: 978-0-615-44323-2

I0191954

Taboo: Untold Family Secrets Revealed

Cover design by MC Brown Photography
Website: www.mcbrownphotography.com

TO ORDER: Go to www.comeoninwithrobin.com

ACKNOWLEDGEMENTS

First of all, I'd like to thank Jehovah, Christ Jesus & The Holy Spirit for enabling me to survive a tumultuous childhood and have the courage to put my experiences into a book. I also thank my loving husband, Cedric, and beautiful daughter, Raven, for their unconditional love and support. I'd like to make special mention of those who were willing to be transparent by sharing their stories. Thank you Crystal, Junwanna and Timeka for allowing me to include your **Taboo** experiences that will help others to heal. I especially want to extend my gratitude to my Aunt Bettye for not only sharing her story but assisting with the editing of **Taboo**. It meant a lot to me. I'd also like to thank Matthew and Paula for their creative genius in designing the cover and offering me support in multiple endeavors. I can't list everyone by name but I also thank others who either listened to or read excerpts of the book and lent a comforting shoulder to lean on. May God bless you all for helping to make this vision come into fruition.

FOREWORD

I saw this movie and began to journal my feelings – something I had never done regarding my abuse. I then shared it with one of my cousins.

She said, "That's a book, Rob! That's a book that's gonna help a million women, at least."

I thought about it and decided she had a point, so here goes. In this book, I've chosen to write about not only my experiences, but those of other family members who have suffered the crime of **Taboo**. I didn't realize how many of us had experienced this until I began to share my personal tragedy.

I've learned that other families have suffered the same shame in silence. I have a three-fold prayer for you which is: (1) that through us sharing our painful stories that you will be strengthened and will know that you are **NOT ALONE**; (2) that choosing to read this book will not be in vain; (3) that you too may be able to unlock the mysteries of your past and change current and future behavior.

TABLE OF CONTENTS   PAGE

Chapter 1 ~ The Genesis: Evil Unmasked

Taboo. The word even sounds foreboding, but what does it mean? The dictionary defines it as follows: *1. A prohibition against doing, using or mentioning something because of association with powerful supernatural forces. 2. A cultural prohibition against some word or act. 3. Set apart as inviolable. 4. Banned for social or moral reasons.*

I suppose that you can think of a number of things that is **Taboo**, but there is one that is probably second on the list only to murdering a family member. What is it? *Incest and child molestation.* The act is so depraved that many don't even want to acknowledge that it exists - let alone that it happened to them or one of their loved ones. The perpetrators pretend that they're not doing it or that it is a mutually agreed upon act. How ridiculous is that? When was the last time you've heard a five-year-old say to her father, brother, etc.: *"Hey let's have sex. I love it when you rub my private parts and make me put your penis in my mouth. Oh and I really like the way you put the pillow over my head to block the screams that come from you* *putting your adult sized penis into my infantile vagina. Oh yippee! I can't wait!"*

Sounds ludicrous, doesn't it? Yet that's what these filthy beasts - male and female molesters would have you to believe - that the act is consensual. **BULL!!!**

The outrage over what happened to me and others in my family and how it put a strangle-hold on our adult lives, has led me to boldly speak out about this **Taboo** subject. I'm willing to disclose our family secrets in the hopes that it will help other women and possibly men to heal. What I'm about to share may bring pain and shame to my family, but if I'm able to help one young girl or boy to stop the cycle of abuse, it's worth it.

****

Let me tell you how this started. I didn't just wake up one morning and decide to air our dirty laundry.

One evening I was watching what was supposed to have been a horror movie. It was called *An American Haunting.* I was enjoying it and remembered that I'd seen it before. For some reason, I'd totally forgotten how the movie ended. To my surprise, the haunting was caused by the living girl's spirit that was upset that her father had brutally raped her. Her senses were terrorized by these memories. Of course the father suffered too, but he refused to acknowledge what he'd done and wanted to believe that it was a witch's curse.

During this revelation, I began to sob profusely to the extent that my nose was dripping. I asked God to let me experience whatever I needed to in order to remember. I'd been reading this book on molestation which suggests that you remember the abuse so you can confront the source of your pain and heal your wounds. I didn't completely agree with this philosophy but decided to test the theory.

As I cried, I wanted to reflect on how it felt when my stepfather used to come into my room while my mother and younger sister slept. There is a scene in the movie that shows the father going into his daughter's room while her mother and siblings slept. Watching that tore me apart. The girl said: *"Mama always was a heavy sleeper"* and so was mine. She was the one who snored and so did the girl's mom.

Later, when the girl made her mother remember walking in on her husband attempting to abuse her (the husband convinced her that she was sleepwalking and imagined it), the mother wanted him dead. The same was true with my mother.

There was a time when I felt my mother had to know. I remember something similar to what the girl experienced. My mother got out of bed and peered into the dark living room. My stepfather was leaning over me while I lay on the floor spread-eagle. Although it was very dark and all you could see were shadows, I thought she still should've seen us on the floor and wonder why we were there. I wanted to scream out to her to come save me and throw him out, but I was afraid of what he might do. Yet, I thought I was finally rescued because surely she would see what was happening without a word from me. Instead, he told her to go back to bed and guess what? She did! I was livid and heartbroken!

You would've thought he would have stopped since he got so close to being caught. But NO! That filthy, depraved, greedy, bastard continued to molest me! I just retreated deeper into myself and realized that help was not going to come for me. I finally began to really believe his threats. I was alienated from my mother and God.

Unfortunately, there were times when my body responded with desire during his assault on my infantile vagina. I remember wanting him to go all the way. Although, later I was repulsed by that, it greatly pleased him and increased his depraved ecstasy. Thankfully, he never went all the way. I've learned not to hate my body for reacting naturally to being massaged in a way that a child never should experience. Yet, it is comforting to know that those times of arousal were few and far between – maybe only three times. Most times I responded with repulsion and indifference. Sometimes I was awake when he would put me back in my bed, but I would quickly go to sleep. I guess I thought he would stop if I fell asleep on him. Other times, I did math problems in my head till I blacked out or went to sleep. I would often wake up and it would be morning – like the nightmare the night before hadn't happened.

I hated him! I lived in horror of the nights and in anticipation of going to school where I felt I was in control. I was a 5th grade honor student and was looked up to by everyone, even 6th graders. Sadly, I took out my frustrations on my peers.

I've always felt that it was my duty to protect others and to never be a victim, but I was one at home and there was nothing that I could do about it. Yet, there was something I could do in school. I took up for other students and meted out "Robin Justice" on those who dared to harm anyone smaller or weaker than they. My friends and I would meet at the "Big Tree" at the back of our school yard. Everyone knew that that was my spot and the only way you could go there was if you were invited or had a problem you wanted me to solve. Quite frankly, I was a bully. I wasn't very big, but I wasn't small and had a hell of a mouth and that frightened even boys! I was a thick, pretty little girl who used my charm to get you to do whatever I wanted non-violently and when that didn't work, I'd use force. Either I'd haul off and hit you or I'd send one of my friends - boys and girls - to take care of my "lightweight". If only I could get someone to handle my "heavyweight" at home.

The abuse didn't start off harsh. In fact, it started off pretty innocently. However, before I go into all of that, let me take you back to the very beginning.

12

Chapter 2 ~ A Glimpse into Innocence

Like many people, I came from a broken home. In November, 1969, my parents married when my mother, Sheila Denise, was seventeen and my father, Darrell Wayne, was eighteen. My father was my mother's first boyfriend and they were madly in love. Unfortunately, they were forced to marry because my maternal grandmother discovered that they were having sex and this infuriated her. She told my mother that either they marry or she'd put her in juvenile hall. For some reason they believed her threats and got married.

A few months into their teen marriage, my mother got pregnant and I was born in January, 1971. My sister showed up in October, 1973. Later, my parents decided that they couldn't make a "go" of marriage and separated.

My mother was a beautiful woman and thus had countless admirers. Some became live-in boyfriends. She had a relationship with a man I detested. When he was home, I tried not to be. I used to love to stare at him with my moon-sized dark eyes while sucking my right thumb and folding my left ear. I used to pretend that I had secret powers and that if I stared at him long enough, he'd die! It brings back a chuckle when I think of my five-year-old fantasy. However, he didn't think it was funny. He used to hate when I did that – it was like he could read my murderous thoughts towards him. Every now and then, he'd ask my mama to make me stop. I would for a few minutes and then I'd start up again.

My mother had our downstairs manager baby-sit me after school. I loved it down there. They were a blended family. The husband was a preacher with two teenaged sons from a previous relationship. They were fourteen and fifteen. He and his wife had a three-year-old son together. The younger of the teenaged boys had my first name, so to avoid confusion, they called me by my middle name, LaTrice.

Since I loved it down there and I was the only girl, I began spending full weeks and weekends with them. I was like their very own daughter. I cherished that position in their family.

Their oldest boy knew that I loved to talk. One time I told him about the fact that I'd heard my mother and her boyfriend making strange noises in their bedroom. He later blackmailed me with that information. I believed that if he told my mama that I was telling her business that she'd spank me and stop me from spending so much time downstairs and I dreaded that. Even though I missed sleeping in the same room with my two-year-old sister, I didn't want to be in the same house as my mother's abusive boyfriend.

I witnessed him beat my mother countless times. There was also a time when he kicked her with his steel-toed work boots. One time, it got so bad that he straddled her on the floor and began to choke her. When I witnessed him doing that, I'd had enough! I was only five but I knew I had to do something to get this animal off my mother. After all, if he killed her, who would take care of my sister and me? I marched into the kitchen and picked up a huge chef's knife. I went back into the living room and stood over him. I said: "Get off of my mama now before I kill you!" He looked up and he couldn't believe his eyes. Here was this pint-sized little girl standing over him ready to cut him from A to Z. I'm sure he had flashbacks of all the times I stared at him with murderous intent.

He asked my mother to tell me to put the knife down. "Not until you get off of her." He immediately obeyed me and only then did I return the knife to its place. I could tell that my mother was impressed yet fearful of my display of bravery. I'm sure she knew how ugly it could've gotten and that most likely we both could have been killed by him, but she admired my guts and love for her. Hell, I didn't know that he could kill us. At that point, I thought I was "Super Robin" and nothing would keep me from defending my mother and killing that jackass! I never saw him hit her again after that. So now you can see where the idea was birthed in me that it's my duty to protect victims and underdogs. I still feel that way and make no apologies for it, although now, I choose more effective means than violence.

I digressed. Let me get back to this boy. So, one afternoon after he'd come home from school, his stepmother left us alone in the apartment. He brought me into his room and turned on some music and said that we were going to play a game. The game involved me "dancing" while lying on my back on his bed. Sounded like fun to me and he knew how much I loved to dance. I knew all the new dances and thought this was a new one I needed to learn. I couldn't wait!

So I got on his bed and tried to "dance". He then surprised me and lay on top of me. He said that he was "dancing" too as he rocked on me back and forth. He tickled me a bit and I laughed. I thought it was a game. What did I know? He never took off his clothes or mine and never touched my vagina with his hands, so I didn't initially think there was anything wrong with it. After all, I was only five and he was fifteen. I guess this went on for a couple months or so when we were alone.

I recall one time when one of his friends rang the doorbell. He didn't let the boy in and rushed back to me. I asked him to let his friend join us and he said no and reminded me that I couldn't tell anyone or he'd tell my mother what I told him about the noises she made in her room. It was then that I became uncomfortable and thought that something was wrong since he threatened me. I stopped cooperating and it stopped as suddenly as it began.

17

I wish I could say that was my only encounter with being molested, but it wasn't. It would progressively become less playful and more brutal.

Chapter 3 ~ Innocence Stolen

My mother eventually left that low-life boyfriend of hers and we moved to another city and apartment. It felt good to live in a house with just my sister, my mother and me. We could walk around scantily clothed and not be concerned about an abusive man trying to call the shots.

When I was nine, my mother met Lester. They met at a house party and it was "love at first sight" for them. My sister and I really liked him a lot. He was handsome. At the time, Jheri curls were in and his was thick, full and shoulder length. He was 5'11" and solidly built. My mom was only 5'2" and he towered over her.

Soon after they got together, my mother got pregnant. I was ecstatic and so was Lester! I'd been praying for another sibling – I didn't care if it was a boy or girl. I just wanted a baby to take care of. Ever since I was seven, I took care of the neighborhood kids and wanted a baby of my own, so to speak.

Even though Lester didn't move in, he was always at our home, the Pendleton's in Southgate. He worked at a department store and showered my mom with gifts for the baby - from clothes to a bassinet and crib. He didn't leave Miko, my sister, and me out. He bought us a new wardrobe of clothes and our first 13 inch color TV to put in our room! That was big stuff in the early eighties. He also bought all the latest albums and my house became the hang out for my booty-shaking friends. I loved to teach new dance steps and since we had one of the best stereos and music in the complex, my house was the place to practice. As you can see, Lester was a wonderful man and for the first time in my life, I actually wanted my mother to be married to someone other than my father.

Tiffani Reshaun was born premature in March, 1981. She was actually due on April 19, (Resurrection Sunday that year). Tiffani was born with jaundice and only weighed a little over four pounds. She couldn't leave the hospital until she weighed five pounds. It was a very stressful time for my mom and me. It broke my mother's heart to have to leave my sister in the hospital. However, the day after my mother had the baby, something interesting happened.

My stepfather and I came home from the hospital to get some clothes to take back to my mother for when she came home. She had a cesarean section and stayed in the hospital for three to five days. After we'd gotten the clothes, he pulled me down on my mother's bed and began to tickle me. He rolled me over onto my back and he lay on me and continued to tickle me. It was fun. Not surprisingly, I didn't think of the game that boy played with me when I was five. I was ten now. It wasn't until many years later that I compared the two incidents. Thus, I didn't immediately feel uncomfortable till I got tired of laughing. He got up and we proceeded to leave. That was the first time that he'd ever gotten that physical with me and I just thought he was excited about having a baby girl of his own. He had two other boys that were younger than me and he really wanted a girl.

I was on Cloud 9 when Tiffani finally came home! I loved her so very much. She was caramel-colored with straight, fine, black hair. She was so tiny and always smelled so good. My mother and I took good care of her. We even insisted that people wear a cloth diaper "mask" over their face when they held her when she first came home since she was very susceptible to getting sick.

I noticed that Tiffani didn't seem as alert as other babies. Remember, I was always taking care of other peoples' babies and toddlers and prided myself on knowing how to care for them like a grown up. Nowadays, you don't let seven-year-olds take care of babies alone in the house but back then, people trusted me with their kids and would pay me a small stipend.

I began testing Tiff-Tiff's reflexes. She rarely blinked. Most people blink several times in a minute. She didn't. It seemed like it would take a couple minutes or more before she blinked. Another thing that seemed strange is that when I put my hand over her nose and mouth, she wouldn't fight my hand, kick and try to breathe.

I tested this other baby I baby-sat and she immediately tried to knock my hand away from her face. Granted, she was about one or so, but nevertheless, I felt that Tiff should have

22

responded, rather than just lay there as if her breathing wasn't obstructed. I told my mother about my observations and she told me not to worry about it. She was premature and would catch up.

I thought she was right. Tiffani began to gain weight and seemed much livelier. She was getting so cute and I thanked God for giving me a baby sister to take care of. I rushed home everyday just to hold my baby.

Tiffani caught a cold and my mother took her to the doctor on a Thursday morning. The doctor told my mother that Tiff-Tiff was fine. He also told my mother to stop letting Tiffani sleep with her. After her early morning feeding, she was to be put in the bassinet that was next to my mother's bed. Up to this point, my mother regularly let Tiffani sleep on her chest or lay next to her after she woke up around 4 AM for her feeding.

The next morning was a Friday; my mother woke up around 7AM and came into my room to wake Miko and me up. She then went back to her room and called for Tiff-Tiff to wake up. Back in those days, doctors told parents to let babies sleep on their stomachs to avoid choking or whatever. So that's how Tiff was sleeping. Usually, Tiff would wake up before we did but this time she didn't respond to my mother's voice.

My mother picked her up and she noticed that mucous was coming out of her mouth and nose and her skin looked greenish and she wasn't breathing. My mother screamed and dropped Tiffani back in the bassinet. I ran into the room and immediately picked up my baby. I cradled her in my arms and begged Jehovah not to let my baby die. Sadly, none of us knew CPR. My mother called her best friend and my grandmother. Someone called the ambulance. When they arrived, they took Tiffani from me and put something over her face and tried to resuscitate her. I remember seeing her little gowned body jerk in the muscular arm of the EMT who held her as he walked her to the ambulance.

On the way to the hospital, I began to bargain with Jehovah. "Jehovah, if You save my baby sister, I will always serve You. If someone just has to die, take me. She's an innocent baby that has never done anything to anyone. However, at times I can be a bad little girl. Take me instead but spare her.

If You don't spare her, I will curse You and tell everyone else to never serve You because You're no good." That was a desperate place and some desperate words for a ten-year-old to utter to her Creator.

When we got to St. Francis Hospital, which incidentally was the hospital I was born in ten years before, I was hopeful that Tiffani would survive. After all, God and I had a deal, right? God answered my prayers and blessed my mom to get pregnant, so certainly He would hear my most recent plea.

The family began to gather in this small waiting room that was set aside for us. Lester comforted my mother as she blamed herself for listening to the doctor and not letting Tiffani sleep with her earlier in the morning when she cried to be held after her feeding. I was blaming that lousy doctor too and declared that we should sue him if my sister died.

After being in the waiting room for about an hour or two, a doctor or nurse came in and said, "We were able to get a heartbeat but couldn't maintain it.

We're sorry that we couldn't save her. Would you like me to bring her in here so that you all can hold her one last time?"

Just typing those words above and recalling them in my head, still brings back the tears although it's been over thirty years since it happened. My sister died from SIDS. She was seven-weeks-old. It was May, 1981.

A few of us took turns holding Tiffani. I held her the longest. *That was my baby.* How could she be gone already? I LOVED her so much and couldn't believe that my time with her was over. I was hurt, outraged and felt betrayed by the doctors and God. How could they let her die? How could they?

I was my mother's right arm. I went with her to pick out the coffin, helped her pick out the clothes and whatever else she needed me to do. Yet no matter how much I tried to be there for my mother, it wasn't enough. My mother fell completely apart. I believe she had a nervous breakdown although she was never hospitalized. A few weeks after the death, I heard her tell her friend that she wished that Miko or I had died instead of Tiffani. I also think she felt that Lester would leave her because she believed he secretly blamed her for Tiffani's death. Hearing those words from my mother tore Miko and me apart. I began to resent her.

After the death, Lester moved in. He was thoroughly depressed. He started using PCP all the time. He wasn't the same person, but then none of us were. We missed Tiffani so much.

I then made good on my threat to Jehovah. I cursed Him out as soon as I came home from the hospital that fateful day. I called Him every name in the book and vowed to never serve Him again and also vowed to tell others not to have anything to do with Him. My sister did whatever I told her to do and followed my example. Knowing this, I told her that we weren't going to be praying to Jehovah anymore. What did it benefit us?

I remember someone telling me that the reason Tiffani died was because God needed a beautiful new flower in his garden. What?!? What kind of sense does that make? I think that's one of the worst things you can say to someone when they lose a loved one. How is it that God (who has everything) needs our loved ones in heaven? Give me a break! That paves the way for people to blame Him and become bitter. It's not God's fault that we have sin and death. It's Satan's and Adam & Eve's. Let's lay the blame where it belongs and try to make sense of it another way besides saying God caused it. That type of reasoning made it easier for me to hate Jehovah, thus making me vulnerable and an open target for Satan and his demons.

I remember some of the words Lester used when he began abusing me. I believe we were the only ones in the house and we were in the living room. I was on my way to my room and he was sitting down. He pulled me to him and sat me on his lap and said: "You know I love you very much, right?" I nodded my head.

"I love you like you are my own daughter. Now that I don't have a daughter anymore, the love I was going to give to her, I have to give to you. Do you love me?" I again nodded yes.

"Good because I love you too. I know you miss your daddy, don't you?" I nodded again.

"I know you do. You know since your daddy is not here and my daughter is not here, we're going to have to love each other the way daddies and daughters love one another." With that, he kissed me on my lips, paused, looked into my eyes for my bewildered response, and kissed me again, while rubbing my behind.

I got nervous and stood up. He told me: "Don't be afraid. This is what your daddy would do if he was here. Doesn't your daddy kiss you on the lips?"

He did but it didn't feel the way Lester just made me feel. I felt yucky and quickly went into my room, closed the door and lay on my bed.

The next time he kissed me, he reminded me that it was just a "daddy kiss". Now Lester had kissed me before, but never on the lips and I just didn't understand why he was choosing to do so now. I wondered: Is he telling me the truth? Is he really just showing me "daddy affection"?

My mother and father weren't speaking at this time; so consequently, she didn't allow him to speak to my sister and me. He lived in San Diego and I don't know when the last time had been since we'd seen him. So I didn't have him to turn to and ask about this "daddy thing". I thought about asking my mother, but she was so preoccupied with Tiffani's death and her own issues, that she wasn't really there for me emotionally. Besides, during this time, I really didn't like her that much anyway.

Eventually, Lester began to touch my vagina and promise me gifts for letting him. He told me not to tell my mother and sister because they wouldn't understand and would just get jealous of our "special love". Soon, his "nice" approach became more sinister. When I told him that I wanted to tell my mother or at least ask my friends if their fathers did this, he told me that if I opened my mouth, he'd begin to give his "special daddy love" to Miko. She was only seven and I didn't want him to do this to her. I was her protector and he knew I'd do anything to keep her safe. He then said that my mother would never believe me because she already thought that I was trying to take him away from her. Later he threatened to kill my sister, my mother and my grandmother – the three people I loved the most outside of my father. So what did I do? I suffered in tearful silence.

Does this scenario sound familiar? Have you undergone or are you undergoing something similar?

Chapter 4 ~ Dealing with the Feelings

I'm not a psychologist, so I don't know all the fancy words for what I was experiencing. I only know that I was traumatized by what was happening in my own home. I was supposed to feel safe and I no longer felt that way. I was supposed to be able to go to my mother for comfort and I felt alienated from her. Sadly, I not only felt alienated from her, but everyone in my little world. I couldn't talk to my teachers, my friends or even my beloved little sister. To top it all off, I couldn't even talk to God because I had turned my back on Him. I hated Him! Could this be the reason why I was suffering? After all, the abuse started after I cursed God. Would He really punish a little, defenseless girl this way? All of these questions perplexed me because I had no real answers to them.

Looking back, I know that that wasn't the case. Jehovah didn't choose to punish me this way, but He did allow it. Why? Why does a loving God allow us to suffer? Allow innocent kids to suffer? Well, it all goes back to Satan, Adam and Eve and the choices they made in the Garden of Eden. When man decided that they wanted to rule over themselves and didn't need God, He allowed them to test out their theory. As we can see from thousands of years and possibly thousands of governments, man has been wrong. God has even allowed us to get to the peak of our intellect with modern technology and still man hasn't been able to tackle the problem of crime, let alone poverty or even come up with the cure to the common cold. Our own failure has testified against us. We cannot rule ourselves successfully and peacefully apart from God. *We need HIM.*

Some might ask: Well why didn't He just destroy Satan, Adam and Eve? Why allow us to suffer for their poor decisions? It was because the answer to three important questions wouldn't have been adequately answered for the angels that were watching and the generations of mankind that would follow. (1) Does God know what is best for mankind? (2) Does He have the right to rule over them? (3) Can man successfully rule themselves apart from God? The only way to answer those questions would be to allow them to try and it has taken thousands of years to prove the answer – No, man can't rule themselves successfully apart from Jehovah, Jesus Christ and The Holy Spirit no matter how many different governments they try outside of Theocracy/GOD-rulership because God really does know what's best for us.

So unfortunately, that means that people suffer – even children. It's much like a surgery. A parent doesn't want their child to undergo surgery to remove a cancerous tumor, but they allow it because the benefits of the surgery outweigh the temporary pain of the procedure. The same is true with God. He doesn't enjoy seeing us suffer but He has to allow us to go through this "surgery" so that we can enjoy the long lasting benefits that will come from living in eternity with Him once sin and death are wiped out.

I've spoken to other victims of child molestation – both male and female. All of them felt that they couldn't talk to anyone about what was happening to them. Unfortunately, when some of them tried later on, they weren't fully believed and were even blamed. This is very sad. During the time that I was abused (1981), there were no TV programs about this topic, or at least I never saw any. I never saw a magazine that talked about it until months later. Had I seen this article when Lester first started molesting me, I could've stopped it earlier because a lot of my questions would have been answered. I pray that this book will help someone who finds themselves in a similar situation.

We've all heard it before and I'm going to say it again because it can't be said enough. **IT WAS NOT YOUR FAULT THAT YOU WERE ABUSED!** If you're reading this book and you're currently being abused, **IT IS NOT YOUR FAULT! IT IS THE PERPETRATOR'S FAULT AND ONLY THEIR FAULT!**

A predator seeks out its unsuspecting prey through various means. Their primary way is to seek out their prey's weaknesses and exploit them. If you're a child, you're an easy target. Why? It's because you're taught to respect and even fear people in authority. So how can a child stand up to a parent, a teacher or even a bigger and stronger sibling? It's very difficult and most children are unable to do it. Would you fault a sheep for being attacked and devoured by a lion? Of course not! So you cannot fault a child, (i.e. yourself) for being attacked by an abuser.

Now we've all heard the argument that abusers were once abused and can't help but abuse. **BS!** The cycle can be stopped. I am making sure that it stops with me. I will **NEVER** sexually abuse another human being just because I was sexually abused. Why? *Because I choose not to.* Everything in life comes down to choice when you're given the opportunity to choose. I have stopped the cycle of abuse when it comes to my daughter. I continue to pray over her and have broken the curse of molestation off her and generations to follow in my family. I will speak more about how to do this in Chapter 15.

An adult can decide whether or not they want to abuse a child. If they feel that they can't control themselves, then they can pray and get help. It's that simple. We don't have to make it complicated. Satan wants to dement our minds and make us think that we're animals and only operate on instinct or passion. *No, we have God-given intelligently designed brains that govern what we do. Let's use them and not feel helpless when we are really very powerful.*

Chapter 5 ~ The Birthing of a Competitive Spirit

When a child suffers from the horrific abuse of incest and/or child molestation, it permanently distorts their thinking. They find it difficult to trust people and begin to see life through distorted lenses. They can no longer believe in fairy tales because they are witnessing first-hand the ugliness of this world. The way they view themselves change. They no longer believe that they are a precious, unique gift from God that should be cherished. Rather, they see themselves as worthless and deserving of abuse. I believe these feelings go across the board for girls and boys. This was definitely how I felt, as well as others that I've interviewed.

I'll take it one step further. I began to feel sexy. What does a ten-year-old know about feeling sexy? She shouldn't know anything about it. But when you're exposed to sex before your body is supposed to experience it, you begin to take on an adult view of things. Although I didn't generally enjoy the act of being fondled and tongue-kissed by my stepfather, I did enjoy knowing that I had power over him. When my mother wanted him to discipline my sister and me, I knew that he would find it very hard to do so when I looked him dead in his eyes. With that look, I would remind him that he was going to want me at night time and that I might put up a fight or even tell my mother.

He rarely disciplined us, but there was one occasion that stands out in my memory. I can't remember the specific thing we did wrong, but my mother gave him the belt to spank my sister. He did so without hesitation. When it came to me, he paused and my mother looked at him and said: "What's the hold up? You spanked Miko with no problems. How come you won't spank Robin?" I sensed that she knew he had a special bond with me but couldn't quite put her finger on what it was. Or maybe she knew what it was and didn't want to face it.

I also looked at him with that look I described earlier. Normally, it worked and he would just talk to me or try to reason my mother out of her anger with me. This time he complied with her wishes. He hit me once very lightly and she screamed at him to do it again. He did and then stopped and told her that he couldn't do it anymore and wouldn't allow her to hit me either. They got into an argument about it.

Later that night, he profusely apologized and tried to explain that he felt like he had no other choice. He didn't molest me that night and begged me to forgive him and promised me that he wouldn't hit me again and would try to keep my mother from doing it also. He felt that if she suspected both my sister and me of doing something wrong, he could convince her to blame Miko instead of me. Poor Miko. Yet, I felt that was the least of her worries. She should be glad I was protecting her from what I went through on an almost nightly basis.

So, back to the feeling sexy part. I also felt that my mother and I were in competition and I was winning. I thought about the fact that my mother was a grown woman with breasts (I always thought they were beautiful and wanted them when I grew up) and couldn't satisfy him. Yet I was able to. Yes, a ten-year-old girl with fat for breasts could satisfy this grown man who had a gorgeous, sexy grown woman at his side. That gave me a sense of twisted pride and led to me despising my mother even more.

She couldn't hold a candle to me. He desired me more than food, water or drugs! I felt powerful. When she made me mad (I remember actually hating her at times), I would want him to bother me so

that I could feel like I had the upper hand. I didn't want him to have sex with her because I felt like he was betraying me and even told him so. This was so twisted! He told me he wouldn't unless he couldn't resist the urge to have intercourse. He explained that he didn't want to put his penis in me because he knew it would hurt me and hoped I understood when he slept with her. I told him I did.

The sickness that is birthed out of this evil changes your roles and confuses you. I now see how it affected me. I liked a married man's attention because I felt like I'd gotten a "one up" on his wife. Then at the same time, I hated feeling that way just like I hated feeling that sick competition with my very own mother. **I want to heal.** I don't want this cycle to continue for me nor anyone else and that's why I'm speaking out boldly about it.

You have read the above and may be surprised that I was so open about these feelings. Possibly, you even felt them at one time or another and never verbalized them nor knew that anyone else ever experienced these sensations. Well, I'm here to tell you that you are NOT alone. Other victims share your experience and also feel shame when they think about it. But still I say, **the abuse was NOT and is NOT your fault!**

As a little girl, you were introduced to the competitive chemistry that exists between women. You can't help that you felt a rivalry between you and your mother, aunt or whomever. That filthy man, who took advantage of your precious innocence, was at fault.

In a later chapter, I will discuss how this competitive spirit leads to a pattern of self-destruction. You will be enlightened to find out how this spirit has infected your life and caused you to make decisions that you may not have otherwise made if you were never abused.

Chapter 6 ~ Living Through the Pain

I recall a time when Lester began fondling me while we were in our complex pool. There were about ten of us in the water and I couldn't believe that he would have the audacity to do this in front of so many people! Or maybe they did see and didn't care.

I'm sure you can imagine how this made me feel. Again, I really began to believe his assertion that what he was doing to me was okay and that even if it wasn't, no one had the courage to stand up to him. So what would be the point of telling on him? Who would protect me and stop him? Here he was doing this in public and at least two other adult men were around and they did nothing. Granted, he fondled my vagina under the water while he was pretending to "horse play" with me, but shouldn't they have figured out that something was going on?

As a child, can you remember thinking that adults always knew what was going on and that nothing escaped their notice? You would sneak and do something and it seemed like the adults always knew and you got into trouble. That was how I felt, so that's why I found it unfathomable that no other adult knew what was going on. Or maybe it was an adult conspiracy. Whatever one adult did to a child was okay to the rest of them because they were all guilty of hurting the children in their lives. I'll go one step further. Maybe those men secretly envied his relationship with me and wanted to fondle me just as he was doing and was operating in a spirit of lust. Do you see how the walls of trust come down and you begin to be suspicious of everyone?

I got angry and taunted him to play with the vaginas of the other girls in the pool. I wanted to see how big and bad he really was. Maybe he wasn't all powerful and above human scrutiny and punishment after all. I wanted to see what would happen if he touched the other girls. Were they trained to allow a man to place his fingers in their vaginas like he told me was proper? Or would they scream and tell someone and he would finally be exposed? So I whispered, "Touch them. Maybe they'll like it because I don't. I just want to be left alone."

Of course he didn't, but I'm sure he wanted to. However, he didn't like me doing that. So he had me to get out of the pool and then we went home. I ran into the bathroom and locked the door because I knew he wanted me. I feared that he would go beyond fingering me and penetrate me. He told me that I looked sexy in the bronze woman's bathing suit I was wearing.

He pounded on the door and demanded that I come out. I told him no and made up an excuse and said that I didn't feel well. He pounded even louder on the door and really frightened me. This was the first time this had happened and I didn't know what to do. We were alone in the house and there was no one I could turn to for protection.

At his persistence and pleading, I finally came out. We probably went through this for about three long minutes. I became fearful that if I didn't respond to his so-called "nice" side, he would get mean and kick the door open and really hurt me. After all, who was going to save me and who cared? God and my mother didn't and they were the ones who were supposed to protect me.

He picked me up and plunged his tongue into my mouth while fingering me while my legs were wrapped around his waist. He wanted me to enjoy it and kiss him back. I finally did because I thought it would hurry the process along. It did, but then I wondered if I really did enjoy it. Ugh! I hated him!

Chapter 7 ~ Self-Destruction

Think about your interactions with the opposite sex. Do you feel that you need to control them with your sexuality? Do you feel like you can only feel and experience "love" by having sex? Do you find yourself attracted primarily to people who are in committed relationships? Do you find it hard to commit to the person you're in a relationship with? Do you believe that you are in constant competition with other women?

While a couple of these emotions can be experienced by women who haven't been sexually abused, almost all of them are felt by all sexually abused women. Why? Just as I said earlier, you were exposed to this competitive chemistry by what happened to you.

Since you're reading this book, you now have the courage to ask yourself the above tough questions and honestly answer them. *It is very important that you're honest with yourself; otherwise the effects from the abuse will continue to control you.* You don't want to be eternally controlled by your abuser. As long as you self-destruct by reacting to these twisted sensations, you're not in power. He is. You need to empower yourself. You *can* empower yourself starting today.

Maybe you never considered these questions before because you thought it was completely natural to feel that way. Scripturally, it isn't. That wasn't how our Creator wanted us to feel. Sin entered the human race and from that comes a harmful, bitter harvest that is most bitter among sexual abuse survivors.

Listen to what the Apostle Paul said about what **love is and isn't** at **1 Cor. 13:4-8:** *"Love is long-suffering and kind. Love is not jealous, it does not brag, does not behave indecently, does not look for its own interests, does not become provoked. It does not keep account of the injury. It does not rejoice over unrighteousness, but rejoices with the truth. It bears all things, believes all things, hopes all things, endures all things. Love never fails."*

Notice that the first sentence tells us what love is and the rest tells us what love isn't. Now I know that as an abuse survivor, the first sentence along with *"it does not keep account of the injury,*

50

believes all things, endures all things" may make you cringe.

What is Paul saying? Is he saying that we're supposed to suffer long and endure whatever our abusers dished or may still be dishing at us? Of course not! We're not sadists. *It means that we're supposed to allow love to get us through some very tough times and not become vengeful, bitter people.*

Why not, especially when that's how we may want to react? *Because it only tears us apart and contributes towards our self-destruction.* Haven't you suffered and hurt long enough at the hands of your abuser? Why continue the process by hurting yourself under the belief that you're making them pay?

Remember the Bible also says at **1 John 4:8** that *"God is love"*. What does that mean? It means that He is the very epitome of love and draws others to Him because of it. He has given that same love to us and showed us how much He loved us by what **John 3:16** says: *"For God so loved the world that He gave His only-begotten Son so that those* *believing in Him might not be destroyed but have everlasting life."* Does this mean that God is a "push over" and people can molest children and commit murder with impunity? No! It does mean that He *will* punish them, but ultimately He is patient and wants all to have everlasting life.

So what does all this mean to us? We're not God and don't want to be. We'd rather hold onto our pain and make the abusers and others pay for what we suffered or may still suffer if we're currently being molested.

Ask yourself: Do I really feel better when I hurt others? Do I feel better when I indiscriminately sleep with men? Do I feel better when I seduce another woman's man? You may temporarily feel that the answer is yes, but ultimately you know that it will lead to guilt. So deep down, you know that the answer to these questions is NO. You need to stop the cycle.

Insanity is defined as "doing something over and over, yet expecting different results". **Let's STOP the insanity!** You've done it your way for years. Now let's try Jehovah's, Christ Jesus' and the Holy

Spirit's or Comforter's way. Let's begin to exhibit the love that God has shown for each of us and then allow that to be our motivation and NOT pain.

I know it's not easy. I didn't immediately come to this realization. Even as I write this, I think it's easier said than done, but it's worth the effort. I am a much more joyful person after exhibiting this type of love than I was before.

I've even learned to forgive my abuser. Forgive??? That seems like an insane thing to do, huh? Yes, a few years ago, I would've agreed. But now I realize the power that comes with being able to forgive even if the person never asks for forgiveness. After all, God has forgiven each of us and it is our sins that put Jesus on the cross.

To assure you that I'm not talking about something I "heard" but something I experienced, I will "fast-forward" and share with you how I came to terms with what my abuser did to me and forgave him.

In an upcoming chapter I will share with you a life-changing experience that happened to me in 1994. For the purposes of this chapter, I will hone in on how that event led me to deal with Lester.

I was hospitalized and during that time, Lester's conscience began to prick him a little. Once I came home, he called me and apologized for molesting me. I told him that if he really meant it, I needed him to speak to me and my therapist. He agreed. Meantime, I told my mom (we'd become really close during this time and I loved her to pieces again) about the session and she said she'd show up too, unbeknownst to him or the therapist.

Lester rode with me to the appointment. After he was comfortable, the therapist encouraged him to tell him how and why the abuse started. He said, "Robin used to wear this cute little "see-thru" yellow gown. Her mom always told the girls not to wear underwear after they took their baths at night so that they wouldn't get them dirty and would be fresh in the morning. So I started to get excited by seeing Robin in her "see-thru" gown and no panties. One time I couldn't help myself. I looked at her breasts and wanted to do more than look. I wanted to touch them and her because she was so sexy."

I was repulsed and interrupted him by stating, "I didn't have breasts! I was more or less flat-chested unless you want to call "baby fat" breasts. How could you consider me sexy? I was just a little girl!"

The therapist told me not to interrupt him and stated that he understood how Lester could feel that way. What?!? I couldn't believe what I was hearing and that's when I noticed that it appeared that the therapist was getting off listening to the story! I surmised that this therapist was a pervert and probably was raping some young girl in his life!

Lester tried to resume his story and at that moment, my mother burst in the door. Now up till a week before this event, my mom never knew the full extent of the molestation. When I told her and explained that I hated and resented her for years because she later married and had more kids with him, she cried and apologized profusely and I forgave her from the bottom of my heart. She was ready to rip his testicles off! They had been separated for three years or so. Thus, when she was given an opportunity to confront him with her newfound knowledge, she couldn't resist. She not only wanted him to apologize privately to me but to her too.

When Lester saw her, he flew into a rage and threatened to kill her if she didn't leave. I told him to calm down because she was my mother and this was my session and I wanted her to stay. He refused to talk with her there and guess what? The stinkin' therapist agreed and told my mom that he would call the police if she didn't leave! I couldn't believe this crap and creep! Up till this time, I really liked him and thought he was on my side. After this, I realized my therapist was a pervert and never saw him again.

My mother agreed to leave and I was done talking. I chose to take Lester home rather than leave him stranded, which is what the snake deserved. On the way home, he began to curse my mother and talk about how he wanted to hurt her. This was when I lit into him and told him off for the first time in my life.

"You ain't gonna hurt nobody so shut up! That's what you used to do when you were raping me. You'd always threaten to kill my mama, my sister and my grandmother if I told. Well guess what? You didn't kill them then and you're not going to kill anyone now. You said you was sorry for molesting me but the fact that I've allowed you to make good on that apology and you've decided to ruin it, shows me you're not sincere. I'll tell you what. **No one is going to hurt me again.** If you or anyone else tries to rape me, I'll kill you and them! I forgive you but I NEVER want to speak to you again. I want you outta my life!"

He was shocked to hell by my exclamation! Months later he tried to weasel his way back into my life. Since my sister and I took care of his boys, he thought he could use wanting to see them as an opportunity to see me. I didn't allow it. When they went to see him, my sister took them and he wasn't allowed in my home.

My mother disclosed to my brothers, Brandon and Mark, what their dad did and stated she didn't want them associating with him either. I disagreed with that and told them that if they wanted to continue loving their dad and see him, that was fine with me. They had nothing to do with what he did to me and I didn't want that to come in between their relationship with their father.

For about two years I didn't communicate with Lester and he was heartbroken. When I finally did open up the lines of communication, he was elated and said, "I'm glad you're back because you've always been a daughter to me."

In August, 2009, he called me and told me that he had been going to church regularly and really liked it. I was excited because I prayed for him to get into a relationship with God. He thoroughly hated God after Tiffani died and blamed Him for it. Thus, he vowed to never serve Him.

I asked him if he was saved and he replied, "Hell nawl! He got a whole lot more work to do with me. I did go down for the alter call and prayed the Sinner's Prayer but I didn't feel any different afterwards. I still struggle with drugs and I curse."

I told him that it was a process and that I was happy he made the first step. I then offered to pray for him and he accepted.

"Father, please forgive Lester for molesting me just like I have forgiven him. Jesus went to the cross to forgive murderers and molesters. Please enable him to transform his life so that he will not go to hell. I know you love him and I love him too. Thank you for saving him."

Lester thanked me for loving and forgiving him. A few weeks later, my husband, daughter and my little niece Yani (his two-year-old granddaughter through my brother Mark) went to church with him. It was beautiful. My brother doesn't associate with his dad so Lester never gets to see Yani. Therefore, he was elated when I brought her along.

During Testimony Service, I stood up and talked about how the death of my sister adversely affected Lester and me. We both cursed and hated God. However, Lester and I recovered from that and are grateful to God for giving us both a second chance. I also thanked the church for embracing him. Many of them came up to me later to thank me for that testimony. Even the preacher mentioned it during his sermon and appreciated me sharing it.

Lester didn't expect me to say all of that and said that I had spoken the truth. For the first time in thirty years, he didn't hate God!

"This is the best day of my life that I've had in years. I'm sitting here in church holding my grandbaby and visiting with you and my other grandbaby, Raven. Thank you."

So I know from experience how forgiveness can work. It can take years, depending on the circumstances, but it is necessary and the following will show you why this is so.

Please pay close attention to this parable Jesus mentioned at **Matthew 18:21-35**, which says: *"Then Peter came up and said to him: 'Lord, how many times is my brother to sin against me and am I to forgive him? Up to seven times?' Jesus said to him: 'I say to you, not up to seven times, but up to seventy-seven times. That is why the kingdom of the heavens has become like a man, a king, that wanted to settle accounts with his slaves.*

'When he started to settle them, there was brought in a man who owed him ten thousand talents (60 million denarii). But because he did not have the means to pay it back, his master ordered him and his wife and his children and all the things he had to be sold and payment to be made. Therefore the slave fell down and began to do obeisance to him, saying, "Be patient with me and I will pay back everything to you." Moved to pity at this, the master of that slave let him off and canceled his debt.

'But that slave went out and found one of his fellow slaves that owed him one hundred denarii, and grabbing him, he began to choke him saying, "Pay back whatever you owe." Therefore his fellow slave fell down and began to entreat him saying, "Be patient with me and I will pay you back." However, he was not willing, but went off and had him thrown into prison until he should pay back what was owing.

'When his fellow slaves saw the things that had happened, they became very much grieved, and they went and made clear to their master all the things that had happened. Then his master summoned him *and said to him, "Wicked slave, I canceled all that debt for you when you entreated me. Ought you not, in turn, to have had mercy on your fellow slave as I also had mercy on you?" With that his master, provoked to wrath, delivered him to the jailers, until he should pay back all that was owing. In like manner my heavenly Father will also deal with you if you do not forgive each one his brother from your hearts.' "*

I know, I know. I may have just turned you off by having you read the above. Go ahead and close the book and take some quiet time to meditate upon this and take as long as you need. You may not be able to read further for a month or more. It's okay, I understand. I was there at one time too. Know that I've prayed for all who feel this way and will continue to pray. **Even though I don't know who you are individually, God does and He will comfort your heart.** However, if you ARE ready to experience emotional freedom from your past now, please read on.

By forgiving your abuser, you're not undermining the pain you've endured. You're validating it and realizing that rather than really hurting your abuser, you're hurting yourself by holding onto it. So begin to let it go. Notice I said, "begin". It doesn't happen overnight. But rest assured, rather than becoming weak, you're becoming stronger and empowered to take back your life and not continue to be controlled by past "tapes". You can begin to run your life based upon the love and mercy of God and can stop abusing yourself and others whom you make pay for what your abuser did.

Let God handle punishing your abuser. He can do a far better job than you anyway. He can punish them in ways you are unable to and give them an opportunity to repent not only to Him but to you. If they reject Him, then they'll spend eternity in hell without you having to for failing to forgive. You see, *God can only freely forgive us by us freely forgiving others.*

It's that simple and yet so complex when we try to justify why we have a right to hold a grudge. Don't be fooled by the devil, your well-meaning associates and your flesh. Jesus meant it when he said we must forgive. That does not mean that we have to be "buddy-buddy" with our abusers. We may determine that continued association with them is damaging to us and choose to forgive them from a distance. Or we may call or write them and tell them that we've forgiven them and then prayerfully decide to not speak to them again. Whatever you decide, forgiveness just means that you will let God handle it and will move on and focus on healing yourself. Now that's what's most important - *getting HEALING not HURTING.*

****

Self-Destruction

Some Steps on the Road to Forgiveness

1. Do not deny what has happened.
2. Allow yourself to experience your feelings and take them to God un-sugarcoated.
3. Know it's going to take time.
4. God will show you the boundaries you need to have.
5. Justice - tell the authorities and find out if the statute of limitations has run out in your state if you feel that's the best way for you to handle this or to keep him from abusing someone else.
6. Realize that your way of showing that you've forgiven this person is by discontinuing your cycle of self-destruction. For example, you stop feeling the need to control men with your sex or distrusting your mate.
7. Don't allow others to put a time frame on when you must forgive - *allow God to let you know when He's given you enough tools to do it*. For example, you may want to build a house but all you have are nails. You will not be able to build a house with just nails. You need the other tools. The same is true with

65

forgiveness. You will not be able to forgive until you have all the tools you need and God will tell you when you do.

8. Don't allow others to dictate all the things you must do that would look like forgiveness to them. Like I said, you may decide to forgive but no longer speak to them.

★★

To illustrate the above points, let me share two real life examples with you:

My best friend, Timeka, thought she forgave her stepfather, even to the point of letting him give her away at her wedding. But years later, she realized that she hadn't changed her self-destructive actions. For example, Timeka continued to mistreat other men, commit adultery and hurt her forgiving, supportive husband. It wasn't until she analyzed her behavior that she realized she hadn't truly forgiven her stepfather who abused her when she was five-years-old.

Once Timeka began therapy and God helped her to heal, she was able to stop the insanity. Interestingly, her relationship with her stepfather changed. She no longer desired to have a close fellowship with him, but found it best to deal with him from a distance. Before she associated with him more and thought that meant she forgave him, but the converse was true. Now that she is associating with him less, she is learning what it really means to forgive.

I have another best friend, Junwanna, who doesn't feel vengeful or bitter. Rather she continues to self-destruct by allowing herself to be used and abused by men who don't care anything for her. I asked her could it be that she hasn't forgiven her abuser? She said she'd never thought of it before I asked her. She said she'd even forgotten his name.

He was one of her mother's boyfriends who penetrated and raped her once when she was nine-years-old. Although she never told her mom, he didn't bother her again. After he cleaned up the blood, he distanced himself from her and eventually left her mom. Junwanna believes that the guilt drove him away.

After I read the above information about forgiveness, Junwanna began to ask God to forgive him and she forgave him as well. She immediately began to feel better. I was amazed! I didn't expect her to forgive him while we were on the phone and then immediately feel a release and peace.

Junwanna expressed herself by saying:

Maybe that's why my blood pressure has been so high. I've often heard that if you harbor unforgiveness in your heart, you can suffer illnesses such as high blood pressure, strokes, etc. I just needed to get that off my chest. I never went to therapy and never considered the fact that I needed to forgive him because I had all but forgotten him. Maybe now I can begin to heal and start treating myself better. I believe that I blamed myself for being molested and thus acted out in school. My grades were low and I didn't get along with my mother. I was also taken care of by an abusive aunt. So since it appeared that everyone who was charged with taking care of me abused me, I believed that's all I deserved.

Self-Destruction

I married a man who was abusive and now that we're divorced, I am determined to demand respect from men and I will respect myself. **I FORGIVE myself because it wasn't my fault** *even though I slept with many different men trying to find the love I didn't get from my mother. I shouldn't have done that, but I didn't know how else to cope with the pain and emptiness I felt as a result of being savagely raped at nine.*

Interestingly, I had a good relationship with my dad, but since my parents were divorced, I didn't see him all the time since he lived in another state. My mother was even jealous of our relationship. Now I'm letting that go and have also forgiven my mom. Starting today, I will move on and be positive about my life and will stop the self-destructive cycle I've been on. **I will heal!**

And guess what? ***You will too!***

Chapter 8 ~ My Developing Self-Image

I really believed that this monster would continue to abuse me with impunity. After all, it had gone on for six months and the sexual abuse wasn't slowing down, but speeding up. At first, it was once a week, but it had gotten to almost every night! I was afraid that one day he wouldn't be satisfied with using his deplorable fingers to fondle my vagina and kissing me with his foul mouth, but would use his filthy black snake (his penis) to rape me. What was going to make him stop? Who was going to make him stop?

I no longer prayed and since I cursed God for allowing Tiffani to die, I didn't think He cared. Hell, I felt that He was the one punishing me and using this diabolical demon, masquerading as a stepfather, to steal my innocence.

I was so fed up with this. I was losing what made me Robin. I was a strong, vibrant, beautiful, sassy girl before the abuse started. However, due to feeling out of control and not being able to protect myself, I was becoming weak and hateful. I didn't find enjoyment in life and didn't want anyone else to have joy either. I resented not being able to be my energetic and optimistic self. I used to love babies, but I began disliking them after Tiffani died. I used to love the attention boys gave me but now I deplored it because it reminded me of this sick bastard. Here are two examples of how I saw life and handled the boys I encountered before and after the abuse.

My mom always assured Miko and me that we were very pretty, especially since we had long hair and we were not mixed. She felt that any boy that we liked, we could have. If we told her we liked a boy, she'd comb our hair and dress us really nice so that they'd notice us.

I remember a time when I was seven and I told my mom about a boy that I liked. She dressed me up really cute in my brown and beige dress with brown tights. She made sure that my hair was flawless. She told me she was absolutely certain he'd notice me and assured me that he already had, but that I just needed to let him know I was interested too.

I went to school and he and his friend agreed to play hopscotch with me and another girl. I think she liked him too but there was no way that she was going to get him. After all, my mother made me look really cute and she looked "homely".

We had fun and I won our hopscotch game. Instead of rubbing it in, I told him that he probably let me win and that he was better at it than I was, although that was nowhere near the truth. I was very good at hopscotch and handball and everyone knew it.

Side bar: I know I sound conceited and competitive. You're right. I was. This was my attitude before the abuse started. I didn't think anyone was better than me and if I ever felt "less than", I'd compete with the person until I won. I didn't compete in everything. For example, no matter how hard I tried, I was never the "champ" at tetherball and I stopped trying. Instead I focused on the things I was naturally good at and perfected it so that I was the best.

When it came to boys, I set my sights on the cutest ones in the school that the other girls wanted and capitalized on the assets I had that were better than theirs. So if both of us had long hair, there was no real competition outside of how our hair was combed. So instead, I nursed the guy's ego and made him think he was only "special" when he was with me. I know this sounds crazy since I was only seven when I really started to compete when it came to boys, but you have to remember who my mother was. She was beautiful and used to getting any man she wanted and tried teaching that to my sister and me. My sister never really applied "the principles", but I was an ardent student of my mom and did.

Long story short: That boy and I started going together that day and every morning, he'd pick me up so we could walk to school together. We also used to love to play "Hide & Seek". We had a good time for awhile.

My mother even let us have a "date". We both lived in the Pendleton's and my mom told me to invite him over one evening right before sunset. She had to take our neighbor somewhere and she took my sister with her. Thus, this left me and my seven-year-old companion alone in the house. I served him some cookies and milk while we listened to music and looked at my family photo album. We focused on my adorable baby pictures since that was the time when I thought I was the most beautiful. My mom came home after about an hour and a half and he went home.

She third-degreed me and was pleased that I had a nice time although I told her that I was getting tired of him. Why? He didn't nurse my ego and "ooh & aah" over my baby photos and he didn't try to kiss me on my cheek. She laughed and told me that I was too much. I told her that I had completed my goal of getting him and discovered he was too boring. She told me to give him a little more time and if he still got on my nerves, to dump him. I told her that I would and move onto someone more exciting and let another girl have my "sloppy seconds".

Later my mother threw me a surprise 8th birthday party (the only one I ever had since we didn't celebrate our birthdays with parties because my mom grew up Jehovah's Witness). It's funny, although my mother was never baptized a JW and did a lot of "wrong", she still had some of their legalistic ways like not celebrating birthdays, Christmas and other holidays.

My mom invited him to the party. He didn't like to dance and when I pulled him up to dance, he barely did anything and pissed me off! Here I am – the pretty birthday girl and there were plenty of boys who would've wanted me to focus on them and dance with them and he wasn't acting like he was privileged. So what did I do? I threw him out and never talked to him again!

When he tried to walk me to school the next day, I told him it was over and that I no longer wanted to speak to him. He told me he was sorry and wanted another chance and I ignored him and told him to go with another girl that I knew liked him. It was the same girl who played hopscotch with us. Interestingly enough, everyone thought she was weird because she was Apostolic and always wore homely dresses and didn't like boys. Well, she proved she was more "normal" than we thought when she took my "sloppy seconds"!

Later when I was in the 5th grade (the abuse had started by then), I liked another boy. All the girls liked him but he was interested in me. I was pleased because I really liked him. In fact, I liked him more than all the other boys I'd gone with before him.

Yes, I know. I know you're thinking: "this girl was fast; she's only in the 5th grade and has already had several boyfriends." You're right. I was "fast". I kissed my first boyfriend in pre-school and had had about eight by the time I got with my newest elementary flame. I never did more than walk to school with them, play "Hide & Seek" and give them harmless kisses on the cheek when they found me.

That was all I planned to do with him. However, he was in the 6th grade and more advanced than my little 5th grade self. His friends convinced him that he needed more than I usually offered. So a group of them dared us to "French kiss". I didn't want to, especially with an audience, and neither did he because he was scared too. Yet, he gave into peer pressure and begged me to try and we did. It wasn't good, but it satisfied the spectators. The next time I kissed him, we had more privacy and it was good. You want to know why it was good? Here's where the perversion comes in.

Lester asked me if I had a boyfriend and I told him I did. He told me that he would kiss me more so that I would really become a good kisser. I didn't want to kiss him more and told him so, but he didn't listen. Needless to say, I did become a good kisser and my boyfriend loved and benefited from my "private lessons". Ugh! I learned how to be a good kisser in the 5th grade because my sadistic, sex-depraved stepfather (the 3 twisted "s's") showed me how. I was so good at it, that my boyfriend stopped wanting to go further because I was so good at kissing him and he accepted my no's and was just happy that I kissed him the way no other girl had before.

I'm sharing these little stories about my encounters with boys and my personality pre- & post-abuse so that you'll better understand how Lester changed me. Pre-abuse, I was always full of confidence and was determined to get whatever I wanted. Post-abuse, I began to die inside and felt that I was powerless unless I used my "sexual charm" to entice males. Before the 5th grade, my playful charm was enough and I always felt good about myself. After the 5th grade, I changed and was hateful and relied on my "sexual charm" to draw boys to me.

Thankfully, I got a handle on this and didn't let it completely rule my life like other abuse victims have done through no fault of their own. This may be what you've used to survive and punish the males who tried to "take" from you.

Instead of allowing them to manipulate you, you learned to use your charm to control them. The sad part is that you only feel fulfilled for a little while and then empty inside again. It's that emptiness that we want to get rid of. That's the reason for writing this book - to get rid of, not only the emptiness for me, but the emptiness for you.

What steps do you need to take? I don't know all the steps you'll need to take to get past this empty feeling, but quite possibly, you've already begun to take them. Why do I say that? Well for one, most likely you're an adult and the actual sexual molestation has stopped. Number two, you know the abuse occurred and you're able to, at least, face that and come to grips with the fact that it wasn't your fault. Number three, something motivated you to purchase and read this book even though you knew it would "open up doors you've left closed" for so long. So that's three steps already. The next steps you'll take may come while reading the book and will continue long after you're done reading it. But however many steps you take to get your healing and end the emptiness, is okay as long as you get **HEALED**. That's what's most important.

My prayer is that no one closes this book and remains the same way they were when they read the first page. We're on a journey of healing and <u>the only thing that is not allowed during this time is to digress and continue self-destructive behavior.</u> *Let's promise to love ourselves enough to stop hating and blaming ourselves* for the initial abuse and any subsequent abuse that came as a result of our self-destructive way of "putting our painful past behind us". Let's face it. How many of our abusers live everyday thinking about what they did to us and trying to hurt themselves because of it? Not many. So we need to stop the cycle. I know I've said this before, but it can't be over-stated.

You know, maybe Lester thinks about what he did to me and that could be one of the reasons that he self-medicates with crack and is just an "all-around-loser". I don't know, but I somehow doubt that he defines his life *"before and after the abuse"*, but I do. Quite possibly, you do too. On the bright side, although we can't change the **Before** and the immediate **After**, we can change the **Present** and **Future**, can't we? I know **WE CAN** and that's what's really important: finding and maintaining joy and peace now and into eternity. We're worth it. How do I know?

Jesus Christ said we are and that's why He died for us. He wouldn't have left a comfortable place in Heaven with the Father and suffer a tortuous death on the cross if He didn't believe we were worth it. No matter how brutal our suffering has been, it really doesn't compare to Jesus' and He ultimately experienced every pain possible to man while on that cross.

Think about it: According to **2 Corinthians 5:21**, He became not only the victim of sexual abuse, but the filthy, depraved abuser in the sense that He became sin. That's why He felt forsaken by Jehovah, His Father. You see, Jehovah is so Holy that He can't even look at sin without being utterly disgusted. Thus, when Jesus became sin, Jehovah had to turn His face away and Jesus knew it. People think it was the pain of the nails that made Jesus ask the Father to take that "cup away from him". No, it was the spiritual separation from His Father that pained Him. Yet He did that for me. He did it for you and He is blessing me to write this book so that you finally **KNOW and BELIEVE that**.

I know all of the above was very deep but my prayer is that we all fully comprehend what Jesus suffered so we can **STOP** blaming Him for our pain and realize that He took on more pain than we can imagine so that we'll never have to experience it again once we're united with Him.

Chapter 9 ~ Ending the Sexual Abuse

Now that I've talked about how I coped, I will share with you how the abuse finally ended. My grandmother, whom all of us affectionately call *Mommy* was a delight to be around. She basically raised me and I always looked forward to going to her house for the weekend. Unfortunately, my mother and she didn't have a good relationship, so they were constantly annoyed with one another.

On this particular weekend, my grandmother asked me to read an article in one of the JW magazines. She later said that she didn't know why she asked me to read it but thought that it would be a good idea. It was about sexual molestation. It was the first time I'd ever read those words. As I read the article at the kitchen table, I cried. Mommy asked me what was the matter and had I ever experienced it. She braced herself for my reply and was heartbroken when I answered in the affirmative.

I couldn't say much, but I did admit that Lester had been hurting me for a few months and that I thought it was my fault because I cursed Jehovah for Tiffani's death. She assured me that it wasn't my fault and that he was a sick animal. She embraced me and called my uncle who lived in the back house. When Lamont came in, he was enraged and talked about getting his gun and threatening the animal with it. I had never seen my uncle so upset before. He was a bodybuilding male exotic dancer and was my mother's comedic baby brother. He was always making us laugh, so when he not only admitted to having a gun, but wanting to pistol whip Lester with it, none of us could believe it!

Here was the outrage and the protection I had been seeking for so long! Finally someone was angry about what was happening to me and had the desire and strength to stop it! I was so happy and cried tears of joy. Not only did they believe me, but they loved me enough to make it stop. In addition, my grandmother and uncle assured me that that animal wasn't going to kill them or me as he'd promised to do if I told.

Unfortunately, I had to go home that Saturday night because my mother didn't want us to spend another night at Mommy's. Mommy told me not to worry and not to tell my mother what I'd just shared. She knew my mother would be very pissed

84

that I told our "family secret" to Mommy before telling her.

We prayed and she assured me that Jehovah loved me and didn't cause me to be harmed in any way and would protect me from now on. She told me to start praying to Him again and I did.

Later that night while I was in our kitchen, Lester came in and picked me up near the stove and told me to kiss him. I told him no and he couldn't believe his ears. You see he was getting bolder. He no longer waited for everyone to be asleep before he'd start his foreplay; he'd do it while everyone was up.

There were times when he'd be laying next to my mother on their bed, that he'd position himself at the edge of the bed so that he could reach down and rub my thighs while I lay on the floor and watched TV! Though I'd move, he never felt completely rejected because he knew I was afraid of him and would eventually acquiesce.

This time was different. I said **NO** and meant it. He asked me what did I say and I replied, "I said **NO!** I don't have to kiss you because my grandmother and Jehovah told me I don't have to and you can't hurt me!"

Those words stunned him and he immediately dropped me. Not only could he not believe that I was being defiant, but he knew the "gig was up" and I had told on him and was no longer afraid of his murderous threats. He rushed back to his room and didn't say anything more to me that night.

The rest of that week was long and full of anticipation. You see, Mommy set up a meeting with my mother and Lester for the following Saturday afternoon. My mother didn't know what it was about, but Lester did.

Strangely enough, Jehovah made good on Mommy's promise and gave me peace and protection. Not once did I fear that Lester was going to kill me, my sister, my mother or Mommy because I told. The only thing that surprised me a little bit was that Lester showed up for the meeting that was held at our house and didn't weasel his way out of it.

Prior to the meeting, Miko told me about a time when Lester exposed himself to her while he was laying on his bed and told her to come lay next to him and she got scared and ran outside. That pissed me off and I told her that he had been hurting me.

She couldn't believe it. I also told her that one of the reasons he hadn't continued to pursue her is because I told him to leave her alone and bother me. However, I assured her that it was all going to come to a halt on Saturday because "the cat was out the bag". She was grateful and couldn't wait for my mother to throw him out once she found out.

During the meeting, I told my mother that Lester kissed me and rubbed my butt. She believed me. I thought I told her about him using his filthy fingers to play with my vagina, but years later, she said I didn't. Maybe so, because even at that time, I'd repressed and forgotten a lot. I also told her what he'd done to Miko and when my sister came out of the bedroom to confirm it, she screamed that Miko was lying because she was skinny and he wouldn't want her. That hurt Miko and she ran back into our room.

My mother told me that she believed me and asked Lester about it. He admitted touching my butt and giving me a smack on the lips. He didn't admit to French kissing. Before I could tell her that he constantly put his tongue in my mouth, arguing ensued between my grandmother and mother. My mother told her that she should get off her "high and mighty horse" because she let my grandfather (my mom's natural father) sexually abuse her when she was a child. Mommy denied it and it just got out of hand and it no longer was about me – it was about them. My grandmother left in a huff and I never really got to fully expose Lester.

Miko and I hoped that my mother would throw him out. She didn't. She told him to apologize and never touch me again and arranged for my sister and me to spend the weekend over my Aunt Bettye's (my father's oldest sister) house and that was the end of the story. It was never brought up again.

The bright side is that the abuse stopped and never resumed. The other good part is that about a month after the "revelation", Lester got a good job and was very excited. He was making plans for all the things we were going to do because we were "rich". He thought he could buy my affection back. Whatever!

But wait! Lester getting the good job was not the other good part. About a month after getting the job, he was set up by this woman when he went to a liquor store to cash his check. She saw he had money and later faked like her car was stalled so he would help her. Unbeknownst to him, she had a guy in the car that pulled a knife on him and tried to rob him. Lester "turned the tables" and took the guy's knife and put it to his neck. The cops showed up and "claimed" they screamed for Lester to drop the knife. It's doubtful that they did that more than once because Lester was under a freeway overpass that echoes and he said he never heard them.

In any event, they claimed they screamed more than once and when he didn't respond, they shot him about 2-3 times and left him paralyzed from the waist down.

That was the other "good part"! I was so elated that he was shot! Not only had he gotten shot, but Jehovah had given me a birthday gift! Lester was shot the day before I turned 11!!! I couldn't have orchestrated these events better if I had tried. Yes, God can make people pay for the harm they do to you better than you ever could.

When we got to the hospital, I softly whispered, "Die. Just die!" He didn't, but his good job and life, as he knew it, were gone. The cops didn't buy that what they saw was an act of self-defense and he was shackled to his hospital bed as a criminal and later sentenced to prison.

GREAT! Although he wasn't incarcerated for raping me, he did go to jail and was paralyzed to boot! I was ecstatic and remember taunting him just a wee bit while he was home about the fact that he could *never force me to lay down for his sick, twisted fantasies again!*

But get this: You know, sometimes the devil does take care of his own because one day while Lester was at home on bail, he was smoking "sherm" or PCP with his buddy, while sitting in his wheel chair. He was so high that he forgot that he couldn't walk and got up out of his chair to get something. He was able to walk after that, although with a limp.

The doctors told him that he would never walk again nor father more children (he still had one bullet near his spine). My two brothers were born after that prognosis.

I didn't get Lester out of my life but at least he was miserable and I remember going to his trial and wanting them to find him guilty. When they did, I was happy and of course my crazy mother was heartbroken. Her "man" was going away! You know what she did? She married him in prison!

Right before he went to prison, she got pregnant with my brother, Brandon, two years after Tiffani died, and married their father when he was two-months-old. Can you beat that? This jackass raped her daughter, exposed himself to another daughter and he beat her – one time even telling us both to suck his filthy penis in a fit of rage and she married him! Was she sick or what?

I really began to hate her. The fact that she allowed him to talk to us in that way, begged him to stay, married him and essentially took care of his every need, made me lose all respect and almost all love for her. She was worthless and I couldn't wait to go live with my grandmother, my father or someone other than her.

But again, at least the sexual abuse was over and I often comforted myself with that fact. I also comforted myself while he was away in prison. I enjoyed not having to look at his deplorable face on a daily basis, although we often had to go with my mother to visit him on weekends. He served an eighteen-month-sentence and was released.

Not only did Lester apologize to me when my mother told him to once the abuse was uncovered, but he apologized again a month later when he was shot. Facing death must've made him feel the need to not only apologize but to ask my forgiveness. In fact, over the years, he would randomly apologize without saying why, but he knew that I knew why. However, he never really admitted his atrocious sins to my mother or anyone else, so it was just a hollow apology. *I refused to forgive him. I still hated him and I would for a long time to come.*

Chapter 10 ~ Adjusting to the Aftermath

Adjusting to life after the abuse wasn't easy, but I was determined to put it behind me – or so I thought. Oftentimes, we think that we've put something behind us, but in reality, we end up doing things to get our minds off of it that can be self-destructive. I'll explain.

I was always curvaceous, but when I got to be a teenager, the "baby fat" fell off and I began to have a "Coca-Cola bottle" figure. While other girls would relish the new found attention, I hated it! Why? I was only twelve or thirteen-years-old and grown men were attracted to me. It's like those sick animals didn't care that I was virtually a little girl. All they cared about was that my body looked like a woman's which they desired.

Determined not to be raped again, I tried starving myself in the hopes of getting rid of the curves. That didn't work because my mother noticed I wasn't eating and literally spoon-fed me. Realizing that she wasn't going to let up unless I ate, I "flipped the script" and began to overeat. She didn't seem to notice that. Eventually, I gained fifty pounds in two to three years! I was fatter but at least I got my wish - the men left me alone! I could breathe now and not be in constant fear of those animals. Unfortunately, that also meant that I had to battle the discomfort of being overweight and not having guys my age find me attractive, but I finally accepted that as "par for the course" since I didn't want to be considered sexy to men.

I moved in with Mommy, who was a Jehovah's Witness, and threw myself into that religion. I was determined to be the perfect girl. I stopped cussing and tried very hard not to commit a sin. Of course I did and that just made me depressed, which lead to more overeating. Life was becoming quite miserable for me. That's not to say that I didn't have any joy – I did, but it wasn't long lasting.

I was also very critical of others and couldn't understand why people didn't lead an extremely disciplined life devoid of fornication like me. This thinking eventually led me to obsessing over any hint of sexual immorality. Don't get me wrong. We should abstain from sexual immorality, but sometimes in our quest to avoid it, we think about it so much that we eventually do the very thing that we're fighting against. I'll explain how that played out in my life a little later.

As a teenager, I was a model of purity. I didn't date anyone until I was nineteen. Thomas, a nineteen-year-old Jehovah's Witness young man I grew up with, asked me out on a chaperoned date. It was uneventful and for the first time in years, I began to develop feelings for a male.

Thomas and I began talking on the phone all the time and he agreed to be patient with me and not expect me to kiss or hug him as we got to know each other better. I was determined to be completely chaste and not commit any sins.

We talked for five months and unbeknownst to me, Thomas told my mother that he loved me and hoped I would marry him. She told him not to tell me this too soon or it would run me away. At times he needed to be reassured that I liked him and I would cleverly attempt to tell him that I did without it getting too mushy. One time he asked me what my favorite color was and I said it was him. He was tall, dark and handsome and hearing that made him crack up. He then asked me how long a person would have to wait to tell me that they loved me and I told him six months. I suspect he filed that information away for safe keeping.

Shortly after this conversation, Thomas suffered a fatal injury at work and devastated all who knew him. None of us expected him to die. It tore me up more than I imagined because up till his death, I tried to play down how much he meant to me. In fact, four days before he was injured, he wanted to take me to the movies and I had plans to spend the weekend with my Aunt Cheryl (my mom's oldest sister) and it upset him and he hung up in my face. That was the last time we spoke and that saddened me.

Thankfully, while he was in a coma, his mother and father allowed me to see him even though only family were allowed to. I guess they knew that I was more than just a "friend" to Thomas. I remember praying for him silently and hoping that he'd recover. Unfortunately, he didn't and I was so hurt that I couldn't go to the funeral. I didn't want to see him dead.

I went into a deep depression. He was supposed to go with me to pick out my first car (a brand new 1991 VW Jetta) a couple weeks later, and not having him there was painful. This was the only car I'd ever had and most nineteen-year-olds would be excited about being able to purchase their first brand new car without assistance from family and I wasn't. I missed having Thomas there to share the moment with. I just ate my misery away and gained back the twenty pounds I'd lost while dating him.

About seven months after his death, I took Thomas' mother out for lunch and window shopping. I wanted to know if he'd ever told her how he felt about me. To my delight and healing, she told me that Thomas loved me and hoped I'd marry him one day. She assured me that I wasn't another "notch in his belt".

Since she knew this, she stopped washing his clothes and cooking for him on a regular basis. When Thomas asked her why she did this, she told him it was because she knew that I wasn't going to always do this for him and he needed to be self-sufficient. I cracked up when she told me that.

She also told me that she was looking forward to having me as a daughter-in-law and losing this prospect hurt her too. I told her that I wanted our relationship to get closer and that I could still be her daughter. Thankfully, we did get closer and I loved her for taking me into her heart and she appreciated how I bonded with her too.

A couple years later, I was hospitalized with kidney stones and she was one of my most cherished visitors. She bought me a comb and brush and I still have that brush – over twenty years later – because she gave it to me.

I didn't date again until I was twenty-two. Jehovah's Witnesses or JWs, as I like to call them, are only supposed to date other witnesses and I broke this cardinal rule. My mechanic was forty-four and twice my age. He was a year older than my dad! He was also a well-to-do gentleman who owned his own business. Nelson let me know that he was interested in taking me out, so I finally agreed to go out with him.

He took me to an expensive seafood restaurant and I enjoyed having someone show me attention. On the other hand, I was feeling bad about being with someone I'd have to sneak around with since I knew the JWs wouldn't approve. Also, since Nelson was twice my age, being with him made me think of my stepfather and I feared that he could encourage me to commit immorality and I didn't want that to happen.

Yet, I was not finding it easy to ignore the fact that I was maturing into a young woman with a desire to have companionship. He talked me into kissing him. He was the first man I'd kissed of my own volition and I was in heaven. I really enjoyed being that close to someone. He told me that he found it hard to believe that I hadn't kissed anyone since I'd been an adult since I made his toes curl. He was certain that we'd get together and we began talking of a future as a couple. However, later that night, I felt really bad for being with him and was determined not to talk to him again. I prayed to Jehovah to keep us apart so I could focus on Him. We didn't talk for four months.

Out of the blue, Nelson called to tell me he was selling his business and wanted to see me again. I hesitated and he told me that he wanted me back and wasn't going to let me run in and out of his life anymore. I was so torn in my emotions because I really wanted him but feared that I would commit fornication and I didn't want to break my promise to God to wait till I was married to have sex.

So later that night, I poured out my heart to Jehovah and asked Him to help me stop self-destructing and make a wise decision. God instructed me to fast and pray for three days. *This fast changed my life forever.*

Now JWs don't believe in that nor do they really believe God talks directly to us. So this was a new experience for me and I did as He said. During that time, God began to break me down to my core and showed me where He needed to heal me and He also showed me where the JW organization or "org" was in error. Just this alone was overwhelming to me. I'd grown up in the org and was third-generation.

Then if that wasn't enough, on the last day of my fast before dawn, I was sitting in my car in a hospital parking lot. I was reading **Joel 2:28, 29.** The org didn't have the correct view of this scripture and they taught that it's only fulfillment took place at Pentecost when the saints spoke in tongues for the first time. Silently, I asked Jehovah to pour out His Holy Spirit upon me. I asked silently because I knew how the devil and his demons operated. I didn't want them to hear what I was praying and try to counterfeit anything God wanted to do with me and mislead me. You see the devil and demons can't read your thoughts (as many believe) but they can hear what you say out loud.

Out of nowhere, I felt something fill me from the crown of my head to the soles of my feet! Now remember - all I had been drinking was water and hadn't been to the bathroom in a few hours. The Holy Spirit was so powerful that it pushed that water out of me and I urinated all over my front seat!

I immediately got scared and silently prayed because I was afraid that a demon may have entered me because the org never talked about anything like this happening. Anything spiritual that they didn't understand was called a demon or mental illness. I hadn't had my menstrual cycle in five months and told God that if that was Him, to let me see blood when I went home. Guess what? I saw blood and was relieved that I wasn't possessed – at least not by the demons, but I was "possessed" by the Holy Spirit! I asked for Him to be poured out on me and He responded. *Hallelujah!* Be careful what you pray for because you just might get it.

On a side-note: my sister and I lived together and we took care of our brothers, Brandon and Mark, because my mother was in a drug rehab. Later that morning, my sister told me she was concerned about me because I was acting strange and hadn't been eating. Miko almost spoon-fed me herself and encouraged me to eat. After being assured that I would eat since my three day fast was over, she took the boys and left.

Soon after they left, I got a phone call from a friend. He asked me if I knew where the card party was and if I was going. I told him no and that I was leaving. I asked him to take care of my family. He was puzzled but agreed to and then we hung up.

About ten minutes later, I received another call and this time it was from my "spiritual father", an elder at the Kingdom Hall whom I used to call "dad". As soon as I said hello, he asked me where I was going.

That alarmed me because I didn't tell him that I was going anywhere so how did he know? I hung up, began to pray and then went to take a shower.

We lived in a beautiful security complex and right after I stepped out of the shower, I heard banging on my bathroom door. Now remember, I told you that my family was gone so who could be banging on my door? No sooner than I slipped on my dress, a man burst through the locked door. I rushed to slam it shut and locked the door again. Who was it? It was my "spiritual father" and I couldn't understand how he got into the building, let alone my apartment! I was terrified and began to scream and beg God to help me because I thought I was going to be raped or hurt again.

Why did I think that? Well a few days later, I realized that the layout of my current bathroom was the same as the layout of the bathroom I had as a kid when I was being molested by my stepfather. Remember when I ran in the bathroom to get away from him? Well having this man, who incidentally shared the same name as my stepfather, bang on the door was more coincidence than I could bear at that moment and it sent me over the edge.

Shortly afterwards, I heard more banging on the door and unknown voices and I became even more terrified and asked Jehovah, Jesus and the Holy Spirit to help me. During this time, I spoke in tongues for the first time – a few hours after first receiving the Holy Spirit! That was something I never expected and the org believed that only demon-possessed people spoke in tongues because they thought that gift ended in the 1st Century.

Now mind you, I wasn't holding the door shut. I was just screaming and slamming my hands on the door. When I started speaking in the "Spirit", I stopped slamming my hands against the door. After God was done speaking through me, I felt a calmness wash over me. It was then that the door swung open.

Guess who was on the other side? Three burly cops that were unable to knock the door open even though my "spiritual father", who was relatively small in stature, did so with ease. I later tested it and saw that I could too. So who was keeping that door closed until I could deal with what was on the other side? **It was the Holy Spirit.**

They immediately threw my arms behind my back, handcuffed me and took me to their car. One of them grabbed my vagina and I screamed at him and he told me he was checking me for contraband. I told him that there was a female cop there and she should search me. They then banged my head against the top of the door jamb as they threw me in the car. I eventually passed out.

What the hell was going on? How is it that cops can burst into my house and take me to jail (or so I thought) while I was minding my business taking a shower? I didn't understand what was going on around me and just wanted to lose myself in The Holy Spirit and ask for direction.

As it turned out, they took me to a mental hospital. That was a harrowing experience in which I saw demons running the show. I heard their voices and saw people who were possessed by them - one was even a nurse. I refused to let them medicate me until they told me what was wrong with me. They didn't immediately have a diagnosis but convinced me to take Thorazine to help me calm down and sleep.

Thorazine made me a zombie. When I noticed the effects of that, I refused to take it anymore because I didn't want to be vulnerable to demonic activity because they pounce at the opportunity to enter an "empty" mind as Jesus stated.

I asked a nurse why I was there and she told me it was because my friend and "spiritual father" told the cops that I was trying to commit suicide. Where did they get that idea? I later learned that when I talked to my friend, he misunderstood what I meant by telling him that I was leaving and to take care of my family. So he called my "spiritual father" and they got the manager to let them in to "save" me. When they heard me speaking in tongues, that convinced them that I was crazy and needed to be hospitalized.

Later I was transferred to Long Beach Community Hospital and it was there that I was diagnosed as being bi-polar. Why? Because I felt God was speaking to me, saw visions, spoke in tongues and felt I had special powers to heal and was excited about being God's vessel. Interestingly enough, these are experiences that true born again Christians have. Yet it's not understood by the psychiatric or non-believing world. Thus, it's just easier to label people *crazy*. I speak a little more about this in Chapter 12.

My psychiatrist told me all these things proved that I was manic and needed to be medicated. In his estimation, the fact that I had just remembered being sexually abused just compounded the need for me to be hospitalized for my own safety. You see, even though I always knew that Lester molested me, I completely repressed the vivid memories and the traumatic emotions I felt when it occurred. Thus, this event brought those memories and feelings back in a horrible thunder storm. Perhaps, you've experienced something similar.

I did begin to calm down after being placed on medication. Because I didn't completely understand all that was happening to me and couldn't make sense of it, I thought that the diagnosis was correct. Thus, I made sure they gave me the lowest dosage possible (the same you'd give a child) and stayed on the medication up until a few years ago when God and *even my psychiatrist*, at the time, told me that I no longer needed to be on it. When you consider the fact that the psychiatrist said I'd never be able to get off the medication and would need it to balance my moods for the rest of my life, *this was a miracle!*

All of these events shaped me into who I am today and has made me look into the deeper meaning of why I do what I do, and by extension, why people do what they do. I believe that we can either grow from bad experiences and be better for it or let them destroy us. *I decided to grow.* Isn't that what you've decided to do?

For the next few years, I was a little lonely and wanted to fall in love and marry someone. That time came in late July, 1999.

Chapter 11 ~ My Life Takes a Turn for the Better

I like Reggae music and used to go to Reggae clubs from time to time. On a Saturday night in July, 1999, I went out with my cousin, Gwen, and a friend. One of the things I loved about this type of music was that a lot of it is spiritual and you can dance to it without having a partner.

I was in a different world when I got out on the floor. I'd close my eyes and be in a "zone". One time, I opened my eyes up and noticed I was the only one on the floor and several men were standing around with drinks in their hands watching me and probably fantasizing. I liked the attention.

On one such night, a man came up to my table after I finished dancing and told me that he'd been watching me and wanted to know if he could sit and talk to me. Somewhere along the line, we "clicked" and I walked to his car and we kissed. He gave me all his numbers and asked me to call.

The next night, I had a good friend over for drinks and uncharacteristically had more to drink than I should have and got "liquid courage". I called his home and a woman answered. I couldn't believe it. She said he wasn't there and asked my name and I said "Tiffani", which was the name I always gave when I was playing around.

I didn't go to work the next day and called him again. I couldn't believe I did so. He answered and told me that his grandmother was visiting and was the one who answered the phone. He wondered who Tiffani was and I laughed and told him it was me. He invited me over.

Well, before I knew it, I fell in love with Cedric. It took me by complete surprise. He was so kind and attentive. About three weeks after we met, he bought me flowers, perfume and gave me keys to his house! That was a first for me.

The drawback was that he had two children and he wasn't a JW. I told him more than once that we were going to have to end it. That hurt him but he told me it was up to me.

At the time, my father was staying in my sister's and my guesthouse. We'd just bought a house earlier in July and our brothers still lived with us. I kept Cedric a secret from everyone. However, I finally decided I'd let him meet my father. That meeting would change Cedric's and my life forever.

Cedric was a little nervous and didn't come immediately into my house to meet my father, so he walked to the park that was a few doors down. When I informed my father, he told me he was going to go find him at the park. Twenty minutes later, I heard them walking down the street laughing. My father and he really hit it off and that in itself was rare. My father normally didn't warm up to people that easy, especially someone interested in his daughter.

The next day, I overheard my father telling his sister that he'd just met his future son-in-law and I couldn't believe it. I told him that I wasn't going to marry Ced because he wasn't a JW and I needed to break up with him soon. My father, who wasn't a JW, told me that we both believed in God and that if I let an organization keep me from happiness, I deserved to be unhappy for the rest of my life. He then added: "Robin, you'll never find a man that loves you as much as I do, but you should marry a man that will try. That man will try and he reminds me a lot of myself."

Those words proved to be very fateful. About a month later, my father committed suicide on Thanksgiving, 1999. He pulled his car into our garage, turned on the motor, prayed and read from Psalms as he waited for the carbon monoxide to suck the life out of him.

I was vacationing in Arizona when I got the news and was absolutely devastated. My father and I had a bond that we didn't share with anyone else. We understood one another even without completely articulating our feelings. I knew my father had been unhappy for many, many years, yet I wasn't prepared for his abrupt departure from my life.

He knew me like a book. I often reflect on the time when I returned home from a 3-day cruise to a freshly painted bathroom. My father knew I spent a lot of time in that room, studying and writing. He had also noticed that mildew had begun to maturate in there. So, what did he do? He cleaned and painted my bathroom all by himself. He had even chosen the right color! I was so pleased and gave him the biggest "daughter" kiss and hug ever.

He then asked me to drink some wine with him. He sensed my hesitancy because he was battling alcoholism. He tried to assure me that it wouldn't do any harm. "After all, even Jesus drank wine. Just share this time with me because it means a lot. You and your sister are going to marry soon and you won't need me much longer. I feel like it's no reason for me to be around." I tried to convince him that we would always need him and besides, I wasn't even thinking of marrying.

My mom agreed that we should honor my father's wishes. Ced joined us since he came over to take me to the airport for my trip to Arizona. My father kissed me and told me he'd see me when I got back. That was a promise he didn't keep and echoed in my head when I tried to comprehend the words, "Daddy is dead".

My sister and I were tasked with planning his funeral. We were twenty-eight and twenty-six and had to do something neither of us thought we'd have to do at that young age. I prayed and asked for strength.   Jehovah reminded me of a prayer I prayed less than two weeks before.

My father and I were talking and he told me that he wasn't depressed but oppressed. I had never heard that before and didn't understand what that meant. He explained that he just felt like his life was a failure and that it was beyond his control – like something was keeping him down.   I prayed, "Jehovah please let my father die. I'm twenty-eight now and I think I'm adult enough to handle it.   I don't like that he's suffering. Please let him go."

The answer to this prayer came less than two weeks later. When I remembered that, I felt better and was able to accept his death with less pain, and pleased to know that he wasn't suffering anymore and that I'd see him when Jesus resurrected him.

Ced went shopping with me and helped pick out my father's suit, along with the coffin. He was a great source of strength for me.   Another thing that helped was my being able to say "good-bye" to my daddy in a way most people don't get to nor would want to do.

I discovered that I could help dress my dad at the funeral home. My mother told me she wanted to help me and it was a unique way of saying good-bye. It was like he was just asleep. I commented that his skin looked so beautiful and natural like he had on no make-up. The mortician told me that he didn't and that they wouldn't put any on him if I didn't want it. I was delighted because I didn't want him to have that "pasty" look. In my eyes, he reminded me of pictures of pharaohs I'd seen when they were asleep. He looked stately and that's how I will always remember him.

During the funeral, I sort of presided over it and it was a real struggle. Jehovah's Witnesses don't believe that women should read scripture and stand behind the podium when speaking to people, yet I had to do it. So to comply with their wishes, I put a piece of paper on my head and explained that that showed my respect for headship. Half the chapel weren't witnesses and thought this looked really retarded.

Before the service and while I was still at home, I got on my knees and prayed that at least one Sweet family member would get the "Truth" about God and

115

become JWs. Therefore, I tried to appeal to them by singing our JW songs acappella with a gospel feel. That ticked off my JW grandmother and she tried to "out sing" me so that it sounded like "opera", something she was used to.

My father's wish was that his baby brother, Kelly who is a pastor, preach his funeral. I honored his wishes. After he was up there five minutes, my JW grandmother led the march out of the chapel, followed by my sister and a third of the chapel. I was mortified and so was my uncle. He sounded too "churchy" to them. I stayed and held onto my father's Christian mother.

The next day, I went over to my great-aunt's house and had a conversation with two relatives who were pastors. During this time, we talked about stuff that I had just prayed about earlier that day. The Holy Spirit fell upon me and I was assured that I was liberated and no longer needed to wear a piece of paper on my head. With that, they laid hands on me and prayed for the Holy Spirit to heal me from any vestiges of the false teachings (cultic spirit) I'd received from the organization and I accepted Jesus Christ as my Lord and Savior.

After doing that, I felt like I couldn't go back and live in the house my sister and I just bought. I kept thinking about Jesus' words to just leave things behind and follow him. I felt like the "cultic spirit" that existed in my home and that organization would snatch me back if I returned home. I asked God should I marry Cedric and He told me I should. So I met Ced at his house and announced that I'd left the organization and that we needed to get married. He was shocked to say the least.

We drove out of town, checked into a room and got down on our knees. Ced asked God for my hand in marriage. It felt like we were the only ones in the world and made me think of how it was when it was just Adam, Eve and God in the garden when their marriage took place. After officiating his own brother's funeral just a few weeks earlier, Uncle Kelly was overjoyed to marry us (five months after we began dating) in December, 1999 at his church.

On a side note: The Holy Spirit led me to marry Cedric quickly to keep my JW family from having me committed into a mental hospital for leaving the organization. Think about it. I left my religion and my home right after my daddy died. They thought I had lost my mind. Therefore, The Holy Spirit instructed me to marry Cedric so that I would be safe and they couldn't override his decision. Until we officially had our marriage license signed, Cedric protected me and didn't allow anyone from my maternal side to communicate with me besides my mother. I'm so grateful to Jehovah, The Holy Spirit and Jesus for warning me of my family's intentions so that I wouldn't be subjected to what I went through five years before.

My life had gone through major changes in just one month and I was determined to march into the future God had purposed for me in my new role as a redeemed servant of Jesus and a wife.

Chapter 12 ~ New Beginnings

Being a newlywed was nice. I had a loving husband who showed me that a man didn't have to be abusive. As you know, I was a virgin until marriage. I made a vow to God that I would do that and glory to Him, I was able to, because HE kept me. I couldn't have done it by myself. In fact, I didn't always want to and neither did Cedric but the spirit prevailed over the flesh.

My introduction into sex was a little traumatic. Why? Well I realized that my power was tied up in my ability to say NO to men and not let them have that special part of me. I didn't do a lot of dating, but when I did, I could always walk away feeling that I had won because they never "got any".

One morning after making love, I went into the bathroom, looked in the mirror and cried. I exclaimed, "My power is gone! He controls me now! I don't like this feeling. I hate it!" This sounds kind of crazy, huh? Yeah, imagine feeling that way.

I put so much importance on remaining a virgin that that became a part of my identity that set me apart from thousands of other twenty-eight-year-old women. How many single women could say that they held onto their virginity until they were that old or even until marriage? There's hardly any in America who can state that unless they were brought up in a very strict home and really took their relationship with God seriously. That is one birthright or inheritance I received by being a JW. To mess up and commit fornication was tantamount to death and I didn't want to suffer the social stigma or more importantly, hurt Jehovah's heart that way.

Therefore, it took me a while to adjust to the fact that it was okay to have sex with my husband. I sometimes felt like we were doing something illicit and then I'd have to remind myself: "I's married now!"

To prove that it was okay and that I could unleash myself from this stranglehold of feeling that sex was wrong, The Holy Spirit allowed me to experience something supernatural.

On two occasions while making love to my husband, I spoke in tongues as I prayed and thanked Jehovah for allowing me to finally marry and experience the gift of marital sex. There really is nothing else that compares to making love and knowing that Jehovah, Christ Jesus and The Holy Spirit are smiling down with approval on what you're doing. It actually becomes a part of your worship and the bedroom becomes your private sanctuary. There's a reason that **Hebrews 13:4** says, *"Keep the marriage bed holy and do not defile it."* God sees it as a beautiful act of worship that only married people should share. The devil knows this too and that's why he does everything in his power to do the very thing that God told us not to do --- he wants to defile the marriage bed. Why do you think it's so hard to be faithful to your mate? The devil is trying to tear up what we even refer to as "Holy Matrimony."

I recall when I was thirteen I decided that I was going to lose my virginity to my stepfather's nephew. We liked each other since we were ten. We were playing "Hide & Seek" in his aunt's house and had just sent the other kids out of the room. He mounted me and we tried to complete the act. It was kind of funny because as much as he bragged about knowing how to have sex, he had trouble trying to figure out how to put it in. I began to guide him and at that moment, I looked beyond the ceiling and felt like I could see Jehovah sitting on His Throne with Jesus standing next to Him nodding their heads "**NO**" with sadness and disappointment. That was more than I could bear and I shouted, *"Get up!"* He was startled and questioned if I really meant it. *"Yeah I mean it! Get the hell up now! This is wrong and God and Jesus are looking down on me and I know they don't want me to do this. I changed my mind. Get up before I tear your mess off!"* Needless to say, he immediately got up and told me I was crazy and stormed out the room.

I didn't care about his reaction and was glad that I made the decision to not have sex. For several years, I planned to lose my virginity at either twelve or thirteen. I thought that was cool because all the sixteen and seventeen-year-olds I hung out with had lost theirs and I wanted to lose mine earlier than they did - I wanted to show that I was "super grown". Whatever! However, after this experience, **I vowed to wait until marriage to have sex** and

NOT hurt Jehovah or His Son again. *The "little fast girl" was finally slowing down.*

I completely changed after that and stopped having boyfriends. Sometime later, this same nephew called himself trying to rape me in that same bedroom while I was home sick from school. I was playing a video game and my pants were unzipped because my stomach hurt. He told me that when he came out of the bathroom, he was going to "get some". I said, "Whatever".

He said that if I didn't give it to him, he'd rape me. I really was like, "Whatever! If you try, I will freakin' kill you. I ain't playin' with you." I believe that besides us, only his aunt was in the house and she was asleep in her room.

So, true to his word, he came into the bedroom and closed the door. After looking at me for a while, he pushed me down on the bed and demanded, "Give me some! You know you want to. We always humped when we was kids. Now that we're older, we need to stop playin' games and do the real thang. You know you want to. I ain't forgot about what you did to me last time. If your conscience bothers you, I'll just take it and then you won't have to feel guilty because I raped you. You didn't give it up. Now come on and kiss me."

Of course it has been over twenty years since this happened and I don't remember everything he said verbatim but this was definitely the gist of it. I laughed in his face. I couldn't believe this twerp's nerve. Although we were the same age, I was heavier than he was and there was no way I was going to give into this little boy. I told him to get up and laughed at him even louder and his little ego was hurt. He told me to "f" myself and I laughed some more because he was shot down and didn't know how to handle it. He never bothered me again.

On a side note: I think it's interesting that I was raped by Lester (though he only penetrated me with his fingers, I still felt violated and raped) and then his nephew thought he could do it. Don't get me wrong, he obviously didn't know about what his uncle had done but I think it's a trip that both of them were determined to have me whether I wanted it or not. Does this mess get passed on in the genes?

Sadly, he grew up to be a loser just like his uncle. Maybe the crap is genetic if you don't break the cycle. Well my two brothers definitely broke the cycle. Both of them are successful, honorable young men....*GLORY TO GOD!!!*

When I began writing this chapter, I had no idea I would say all of this but I prayed and this was what The Holy Spirit wanted to be printed. I didn't write this to make you think that I'm "holier than thou". Far from it! I have some skeletons I'm going to let out of the closet in an upcoming chapter that is a MAJOR reason why I'm writing this book. This is just laying the foundation for that.

I know that our spiritual lives affect our physical and personal lives. No matter how much we try to run away from our relationship with God, He ultimately is who we need to *run to*. Therefore, by breaking apart the dynamics of spirituality and faith, I'm helping you to deal with your issues head on.

As sexual abuse survivors, we've established that we use sex to control men and to show and get love to the detriment of ourselves. In some instances, some women have given up on men altogether and become lesbians. It's funny. Gay men will always say that they're born that way. Rarely, if ever, have I heard women say that. They mostly say that they were abused by men either in childhood or adulthood and are tired of their crap and refuse to take it anymore. My aunt will talk to you more about how those dynamics work in a future chapter.

****

Meanwhile, I'm going to share with you how the year 2000 was really a New Millennium for me. A lot of things changed for me. It was the beginning of the best part of my life! I got liberated from cultic bondage and could finally become the woman and **DAUGHTER OF GOD that HE DESIGNED me to be!** All the fear, pain and anguish I went through as a child served a purpose. **Romans 8:28** says in essence that *"all things work for the good of those who love Him and are called for His purpose."* I'm a living testimony of this and I'm sure you are too!

Although I enjoyed being married to Cedric, it did come at a price. Since he was not a JW, my JW family members initially rejected him and held him responsible for me leaving the organization. As mentioned earlier, I decided or rather *Jesus chose to have me leave the organization* back in December, 1999. I wanted to fade off the scene without a fuss but some of the elders (equivalent to pastors) at the Kingdom Hall weren't having that.

One began to harass me at work by calling me and demanding that I meet with them. On a side note: this man and I were secretly attracted to each other. Although he was married, and I tried to view him as my big brother, he would try to slyly take it to another level. One of my teenage guy friends told me that while a bunch of men from the Hall were watching a football game, they began talking about whom they were attracted to in our congregation. This elder said that if he weren't married, he'd want to marry me because he thought I was pretty and loved my big breasts – something his wife didn't have. I was surprised he admitted this publicly, but I have to admit I was flattered.

One night I gave a party at a hotel and he and his wife came. She and I really liked each other and I was determined to respect her and not ever give her a cause for alarm. I suppose that wasn't uppermost on his mind. When they arrived and I went to greet them, he hugged me tightly, kissed me on my cheek, told me how beautiful I was and gazed into my eyes to gauge my reaction. I was stunned and didn't know how to react.

His wife looked like she had just been slapped in the face and was visibly hurt. I hugged her and then took her aside to introduce her to people that she didn't know. I wanted to show her that that meant nothing to me and that I was more interested in her being there than him. She seemed to appreciate that and never treated me like I was out to get her man.

He tried some mess again after that. He was about 6'3" and often tried to look down my blouse if I showed even a hint of cleavage. I tried to wear safety pins in my blazer/blouses to hide cleavage but he could pierce through that. At first I thought he just had a problem with eye contact, but my best friend told me I was being naïve because she was closely monitoring our conversation and how he looked at me or "the twins". She could tell that he was trying to see more skin. Another time he told me that I had pretty feet while we were out in field service (knocking on doors to witness to others). I then asked him did he view me as a sister and he said yes and told me that was why he often hugged and kissed me. I tried to buy that. I didn't have a big brother and always wanted one. Thus, I regularly sought out men that I thought were "safe" to fill that void. I was beginning to wonder if he was really safe.

The straw that broke the camel's back and made me realize that I had to distance myself from him happened at one of our circuit assemblies. This was a large gathering of congregations at a place that we only went to twice a year. We single women always went out of our way to look extra beautiful because we could probably meet our future husbands there.

I was wearing this beautiful navy "car wash" dress. It had a split in front of each knee (or a little above it) and looked like the flaps in car washes. I really thought I looked sexy in it and it complimented my size 20 figure. Most of my weight was carried in my hips, butt and thighs and I had a small waist and large breasts. I looked like an oversized version of

129

a coke bottle. Men who loved full-figured women were instantly attracted to me in that dress. Unfortunately, no single man came up to me but I did catch the immediate attention of this particular elder.

After the assembly was over and I was walking towards my car, he called out my name and demanded that I come speak to him. I spoke to his wife and then he lit into me. "Why are you looking sexy like that? I could see your thighs a mile away! When a man is looking at you, all he can think about is what he'd like to do with you. Don't wear that dress again."

I couldn't believe what he was saying and how he was saying it. I immediately picked up on the fact that he was speaking for himself and no one else. His wife was embarrassed and a little hurt by his words to me. She tried to stop him but he continued and said more than I'm able to remember. It was a good five minutes of him telling me how I looked and how it would make men feel.
One of my friends overheard what he said and felt he had crossed the line and disrespected his wife with his lust for me. You could tell that his wife

knew that he was speaking about his own attraction to me and more concerned that some other man would get what he couldn't have and wanted me to continue to hide it. She used to be a very strong woman like me, but while married to him, she just diminished and only lived to please him and he abused her emotionally.

A few days after this incident, I went to their house for the weekly Bible study with about fifteen other JWs. He wanted me to continue to come to his study rather than another one that I went to at the Kingdom Hall. After that night, I decided against it. I didn't want to subject his wife to his open attraction and lust for me. I loved her. I also didn't like the fact that sometimes I was flattered when I should have been repulsed. After the meeting was over, they invited me to stay for alcoholic drinks. I didn't like what he served and opted for soda.

I asked them would they be chaperones for me and this brother I was interested in who went to another Hall. He wanted to take me to Vegas and I wanted them to come along. He was a ministerial servant which is equivalent to a deacon. This elder said they would go.

We began to talk about what made him marry his wife and he told me that the only thing that attracted him to his wife was that she was pretty. She tried to smile but her eyes became teary. She knew that her beauty would fade and if that was his only attraction, he could soon be distracted by another pretty woman. He then stood up and put his leg on his chair that was across the table from me and positioned his groin so that it was at my eye level as if to state that that could be mine. I turned away. He said other inappropriate things and I left.

I told my guy friend, the ministerial servant, what was said at the assembly and at this elder's house. He told me that he wanted to see this dress to determine if indeed it was too sexy and told me to curtail my association with this guy. He told me that he thought that this elder was attracted to me and didn't see me as a sister. He said that since what he did was right in front of his wife and could easily be explained away as brotherly concern, *though it truly wasn't*, there was nothing I could do but stay away because the other elders wouldn't believe that he was making passes at me. I listened to him. Needless to say, that couple didn't chaperone our trip to Vegas and he and I decided it was best not to go alone.

So getting back on track again and fast forwarding to February, 2000, I was tired of being harassed by this elder and agreed to meet with him and two other elders for what is called a "committee meeting". This is held to determine if a JW has crossed immoral boundaries and need to either be placed on reproof (have limited privileges at the Hall) or dis-fellowshipped (kicked out and no one can speak to you in or outside of the Hall – not even family and friends).

I prayed & fasted and Cedric took me to meet the elders. They wanted to know why I married this "wordly" man and wanted to ascertain if we committed fornication. Earlier we had engaged in heavy petting and I told a couple elders that a few months before. Thus, when I got married "out of the blue", they wanted to know what was going on. Noting that my father had died just a few days before I married him, they wondered about my mental health and if distress or a pregnancy had caused me to marry this man.

After moving beyond that and assuring them that we hadn't had sex prior to marriage and that I wasn't pregnant, I turned the conversation to why I no longer wanted to be a JW. My sister and close friends (your own family members and friends can transform into Judases and the Gestapo and report on you if you're not "towing the line") told them that I was speaking against the organization. The elders told me that I was known for doing a lot of research and impressed them so much that they often came to me for answers on understanding the deeper things of the Bible. Thus, they couldn't understand how I could walk away from the "Truth".

I explained that it was because of my research of the Bible along with Watchtower (WT) literature that I realized that this was not the "Truth". I then gave them several examples of WT false prophecies and false interpretations of scriptures and took them to **Deuteronomy 18:20-22**. This says in essence not to be afraid of anyone calling themselves a prophet, whose prophecies had been proven to be false and that they were to be put to death. The organization had often referred to themselves as prophets.

I told them that I no longer feared them or the organization and gave them my letter of resignation or disassociation.

Do you know how you can tell if you're in a cult? It's when you can't leave with your good name intact. You either have to believe everything they teach and isolate yourself from anyone or anything that teaches you differently or you're dis-fellowshipped. You can't simply walk away and still be thought highly of. They have to malign your name to keep others from associating with you and becoming enlightened.

I wouldn't give them the satisfaction of dis-fellowshipping me and making others believe that I had committed fornication, which is the number one reason for being kicked out. By disassociating myself, I was stating that I no longer "wanted to play with them" and that I had scriptural grounds for leaving and that it wasn't because I was morally bankrupt.

Interestingly enough, after I thoroughly expressed why I was leaving, one of the elders, whom I deeply respected, stated that he hoped that I found the "Truth" outside of the WT because he didn't and wished me the best. The elder who was attracted to me, was silent and visibly full of anger with me. He could barely look at me and when he did, there wasn't love in his eyes. It was like he couldn't believe that I had left the organization *and him* for Cedric. He was like a man scorned.

I never stepped foot in that Hall again and a week later they announced: "Robin Sweet has disassociated herself from the Christian congregation of Jehovah's Witnesses." I was told that that announcement was met with a lot of crying (even the elder reading it, the one I really respected and liked, was fighting back tears as his voice trembled) and several people couldn't stay for the rest of the meeting. They couldn't believe that one of the strongest, spiritual sisters left their ranks. Women can't be pastors or hold any office in the organization, but it was the general consensus that if I were a man, I would have easily become an elder. So it really shocked them that I would leave.

They were heartbroken and confused. I was also heartbroken. I didn't want to leave in this way. I just wanted to stop going to meetings and still associate with other JWs. However, the brothers wouldn't allow that because I was too influential and could easily convince others to believe that this wasn't the "Truth" and there would be others that would leave. Thus, they made me make a decision.

Prior to this meeting, I went to my maternal grandmother's home. She made Ced stay in the living room, took me to her bedroom, closed the door and demanded that I remain a JW. I did the unthinkable and told her "NO". I had never defied her before and this angered and dismayed her. She said, "I don't know you! Give me my key and get out of my house. You're no longer welcome here!"

This hurt me more than words can express. My grandmother meant the world to me and raised me for most of my life. I never wanted to disappoint her. Many in the family would say that I was her favorite grandchild and she had high hopes for me in the organization. Leaving it crushed and embarrassed her. We didn't speak for a year. The devil thought that would break me and make me go back to the organization but he was sadly mistaken. *I was determined to pick up my cross and follow Jesus wherever He led me.*

Jesus promises: *"Truly I say to you that no one has left house or brothers or sisters or mother or father or children for my sake and for the sake of the good news who will not get a hundredfold now in this period of time, houses and brothers and sisters and mothers and children and in the coming system of things everlasting life."* ~ **Mark 10:29-30**

Although I disassociated myself and wasn't dis-fellowhshipped, the consequences are still the same. I lost family and friends. Half of my family and all but one friend refused to speak to me. The JW family members who still speak to me, do so sporadically. Their love for me makes it hard for them to totally cast me aside but I never know when they're going to tell me that they have to put Jehovah and the organization first and stop speaking to me. My sister and grandmother go back and forth with this. Though it hurts, I understand and hold onto Jesus' words above. **He has been faithful.**

I gained three houses for leaving the one house and other sisters and brothers who will be a part of my life eternally. One day my JW family will be saved. God has assured me of this. Thus, I don't worry that they'll go to hell. Instead, I move on to complete the assignment Jehovah has for me and trust that He will take care of my family as I take care of His.

Needless to say, Ced and I grew really close during this time because he was almost all I had. My mother still was close to me since she never became a JW and was the renegade daughter. She lived on my grandmother's property in her back house. My mother told her mother off for disowning me and told her that she would never be a part of a religion that divided families.

When I went to visit my mother, my grandmother would peep out her window and watch me go to my mom's. I knew she was hurting and wished she could embrace me but her pride and religion prevented her until I got pregnant about a year later. Then she embraced me again for awhile and fell in love with my little Raven, who was born in December, 2001.

Sadly, my mother battled with lupus for over twenty years and that prevented her from successfully battling the lung cancer that took her out less than a year after diagnosis. She always wanted a grandchild and used to joke, when I was single, that I should go out and have a baby and she would take care of it. I told her I couldn't because I valued my relationship with Jehovah too much and didn't want to hurt Him. She said, "Oh well don't worry about that. He'll forgive you and so will I." I told her that she was crazy and having her forgiveness was the least of my concerns. We'd laugh and drop the subject until she brought it up again when she began yearning for a grandchild.

When we found out I was pregnant on Resurrection Sunday, 2001, she and my husband were overjoyed! Ced fell to his knees, hugged my legs and kissed my arm that embraced him. Mama lived until Raven turned three-weeks-old. That broke my heart. Raven looked like my mom for the first two years of her life and it hurt that my mother always wanted a grandchild and now was gone and couldn't enjoy her. I look forward to the resurrection where my mother and father will meet their first grandbaby. **Thank you Jehovah, Christ Jesus and Holy Spirit for that hope.**

So much had changed in my life and I was glad that everything that happened in my past prepared me for my present and future. The birth of Raven was further proof that Jesus was able to make good on His promise in **Mark 10.** *Cedric and Raven became the family Jesus gave me for leaving all for His sake. It was a more than equitable trade off and prepared me for the ministry ahead.*

He told me that He wanted me to begin ministering to ex-JWs and eventually open up **"Houses of Refuge"** for those leaving the organization that would leave everything behind and be destitute. Many work for JWs and their only family and friends are JWs. When they take a stand for Jesus, they'll lose all – even their children. I haven't opened up a house yet, but when the time comes for the mass exodus of ex-JWs, I'll be ready.

The other ministry He has me focusing on is ministering to Kenyans both spiritually and professionally. In April, 2009, (along with celebrities and others involved in community outreach), I received the *"African Focus Goodwill Ambassador Award"* for raising approximately $4,000 for 300 Bibles in Luo, Swahili & English and matching 40 American mentors with 40 adult Kenyan mentees. The vision is to encourage them to use their God-given talents to get themselves out of poverty. Thus, the Americans will help them to write business plans and do research to assist them with their various entrepreneurial goals. So rather than *"giving them fish, we're teaching them how to fish"*.

Jehovah also gave me a cable talk show that focuses on daily struggles and accomplishments, while highlighting God's perspective on the issues being discussed. This show is my passion and an example of how God can give you even the unuttered desires of your heart. **(Psalm 145:16)**

When I was sixteen, I would come home from school and watch a talk show and dream about hosting my own show. However, I knew that this would never happen because I was a JW and they don't believe in you doing anything extracurricular that could take your focus off their agenda – knocking on doors until Armageddon comes.

They even strongly discourage going to college or participating in sports. If possible, they discourage you from working a full-time job and encourage you to knock on doors full-time. This pressure led to me denying myself the opportunity of getting a degree, which was something I always wanted but would have made the organization look down on me.

Thus, I gave up my aspirations of becoming an attorney, becoming a published author and anything that expressed my God-given natural talents. I wrote two novels but never published them and just read them to a few friends for entertainment. So writing **Taboo is a huge accomplishment** and one more oppressive, cultish weight I've thrown off me. *Hallelujah!*

I said all the above to say that I NEVER voiced my desire to have a talk show to Jehovah. However, in June, 2001, He opened up the door for me to host and produce my own talk show. When I asked him why, He said: *"I knew this was always your desire and although you never asked me for it, I wanted to keep my Word in Psalm 145:16 and satisfy your desires since you satisfy mine unselfishly. I love you. "* Needless to say, those Divine Words blessed my soul.

After six years of programming, the show ceased airing in September, 2007 – the very same day that I landed in Kenya. While there, God used me to speak my first sermon called, *"He Came to Set the Captives Free"*. This message was in harmony with **Luke 4:16-18 & Matthew 25:14-33**. The Kenyan Vision started here as I aligned myself with the dream of Bishop Juma, of Umoja Village. Incidentally, The Holy Spirit told me to suggest this name to Bishop Juma in place of the name it currently had which meant "envy". In contrast, Umoja means "unity". This was in answer to Juma's prayers and we renamed the village.

Being in Kenya, reminded me of the vision God gave me thirteen years before when I first received The Holy Spirit in 1994. He showed me a vision in which I was ministering to Africans but I didn't know what country I was in or who I was speaking to in particular. I just saw me speaking to a room full of people and yearned to fulfill it. While at the pulpit,

God reminded me of this vision and I began crying and rejoicing in the Lord! You see, the doctors were wrong. God really gave me a vision. It wasn't a delusion as they claimed. God fulfilled it years later! *God is GOOD and He will always make good on His promises.* We just need to make good on our promises to Him.

During this visit, God showed me that He wanted me to become an ordained minister. I fulfilled His desire and was ordained as an Elder/Evangelist in August, 2008. Prior to this, I gave my first sermon in America in April, 2008 called, *"Know the Spirit You're Working With".* This sermon highlighted the various ways the devil can come against you – even using mental illness to make you think you're not really hearing from Jehovah, The Holy Spirit and Christ Jesus. Again, this message was birthed out of what happened to me back in 1994. Many came up to me afterwards and told me they'd never heard a sermon so real that dealt with real issues and warned them that Satan would begin using the world to label *"true, born again, sold-out-for-Jesus-Christians"* mentally ill in order to keep others from taking their message seriously.

145

In August, 2009 (two years after going to Kenya and aligning myself with Bishop Juma), The Holy Spirit gave me another message entitled, *"A Dream Deferred"*. This is taken from **Genesis 37-50**, in which Joseph dreamed 2 dreams that led to his slavery and incarceration. He could have thought that his dreams of rulership would never happen because his circumstances had declined drastically since receiving the dreams. He then had the opportunity to interpret the dreams of two servants of the pharaoh and the pharaoh himself. His being willing to interpret their dreams, even though his hadn't come to pass, led to his dream finally being fulfilled --- 22 years after Jehovah first gave him his dreams!

He had me to give this sermon at my uncle's church retreat; someone was so blessed by the message that she had me give the message on her internet radio program in September, 2009! Thus, more people than I initially envisioned were blessed by God's encouragement.

The Holy Spirit told me that sometimes He will *"defer our dreams"* so that we can align ourselves with others and help their dreams come to pass.

Our being willing to do this unselfishly will lead to our own dreams' fulfillment! He told me that since I had been faithful in assisting Juma and other Kenyans with their dreams, He would bless me to get my talk show back on the road again and bountifully bless it. Hence *"A Dream Deferred"* can lead to countless blessings beyond our wildest dreams! Stay encouraged reader.

I hadn't intended to record any of this. In fact, when I woke up before dawn with the push from The Holy Spirit to write, I thought I was going to begin my next chapter, but He had another purpose. *He wanted me to enhance this chapter more and encourage you to hold onto the dream he gave you because He will bring it to fruition.* **You just need to HOLD ON and TRUST HIM.**

So in accordance with God's Will, **I am living a full and prosperous life.** *I am moving full speed ahead to put God first in ALL things.* Yes, **the New Millennium has been good to me.** Yet, things haven't always gone smoothly. It wouldn't be life on earth if it did. The next chapter will show how even the best laid plans can have hiccups. Yet we are to put our faith in God, overcome our temptations and resist allowing our visions/dreams to become derailed.

Chapter 13 ~ A Rude Awakening

Being overweight for all of my adult life took its toll on my self-esteem. As any woman can testify, we put a lot of our self worth into our looks and how others view us. We may try not to let our looks effect us, but it does from time to time. So if we feel beautiful and others compliment us, we have a good day. If the reverse is true, we have a bad day.

Ced noticed and loved me while I was overweight and that really served to boost my esteem. Now don't get me wrong. Most people didn't even know that I had low self-esteem when it came to my looks. I didn't carry myself as a victim, but I knew that I missed having men view me as attractive. I no longer feared men as I had before when I decided it best to gain weight to make them ignore me. Thus, I noticed that unless a man was into "big women", he didn't look twice at me.

During one of my periods of feeling "ugly", I went to Jamaica for about five days with my aunt, Muriel. While shopping for this trip, I hated that all the clothes I bought were a 3X. That sickened me!

Thus, imagine my surprise when I arrived in Jamaica and men were checking me out! I couldn't even leave the airport without them telling me how beautiful and desirable I was!

Once I got to our resort, the attention intensified to the point of intoxication! I hadn't had that much attention since I was thirteen or maybe ever! Now I know these men were probably trying to find a way to either "hit-it-and-quit-it" or find a wife to take them back to the States, but the attention still felt GREAT!

I almost forgot I was married. I sort of went into a "make believe world" and reveled in the attention. On my first night there, a young man with beautiful caramel skin and dimples (I'm a sucker for dimples) approached my table. He worked in Housekeeping at the resort and one of the women that my aunt and I were sitting with, beckoned him. She inquired about some other guy and he answered her. Meantime, instead of walking away, he focused his attention on me.

That tickled me because I thought he was a little boy. I asked him how old he was and he said, "Old enough to teach you a few things." Muriel, the other woman and I cracked up. I asked him what year he was born in and it turned out he was only six years younger than I. He asked for my room number and I gave it to him. He finally left the table and soon he was "out-of-sight-out-of-mind."

Later that night I went Reggae dancing at a club at the resort and danced with a bartender. Another guy who worked there was trying to make his move on me and he annoyed me. Finally, I made it back to my room and my aunt said that the guy in Housekeeping called. I'd forgotten all about him and was a little tickled by him calling so quickly.

After we finished sightseeing the next day, I chatted with a cute bartender named Hezekiah who reminded me of Thomas, the young man I dated that died. He was sweet. I told him that I was interested in seeing the nightlife off the resort but my aunt was too tired to go. He said he would love to take me but couldn't because his girlfriend would be expecting him home. However, he suggested that I go with the guy in Housekeeping because he was trustworthy and wouldn't harm me. I'd forgotten his name and he reminded me that it was Orlando. I was surprised that he spoke highly of this guy when it seemed like most of the men that found me attractive were acting like rivals.

Later on at dinner, one of the waiters told me I was beautiful and had pretty feet. He offered to take me out and I told him I'd think about it. Later, when I didn't go out with him, he fussed at me and told me not to return to his restaurant. I laughed and walked off unbothered by his anger. Another waiter brought me a lollypop and told me that I was so sweet that he wanted to let me know how much. I thought that gesture was cute even if it was a little corny.

During dinner, I needed to go to the restroom and while on my way, I ran into Orlando. We hugged and he told me he had been looking for me and asked if he could take me to the casino after he got off work. I told him yes and mentioned that a bartender suggested I go out with him. He was surprised and said that just proved we were supposed to have fun together.

We agreed to meet at one of the bars at the resort. While I was at the bar, there was another bartender, Samson, who was easy on the eyes. He thought I was nice looking too and we chatted a bit. The manager of the bar liked my aunt and we talked about her and other stuff when Samson was serving drinks. Meantime, Orlando came to the bar and whispered something to Samson and they looked over at me. Then Orlando told me he'd see me later and left. When he came back, the manager distracted the bartender so that I could leave.

It wasn't until later that I found out that Orlando whispered to Samson that I was the woman he'd told him about and to stay away from me. The manager was a friend of both guys and knew that both were pushing up on me. Later he told me that he didn't want Orlando to get his feelings hurt and would rather I talk to him over Samson. Needless to say, Samson just pushed up on me more the next day and gave me his number but I never called him. When I told Orlando, he was ticked off because he thought they had an understanding.

Now I know you're thinking: You're married. What is your problem? I totally agree. My husband and I didn't wear our rings - he lost his and mine needed to be repaired. So I didn't have on a ring and I really slipped into this "make believe world". Though I hung out at the bar at night, I never had more than one drink, so I can't say I was drunk. It was like a cloud of lust hung over me and I liked being desired by all these men and teasing them. My mom used to call me a "DT or dick tease" and I was truly that. I would talk a good game but would never do anything. So I had relapsed into that. I was just having some fun and letting off steam and stress.

My husband and I had been married almost five years and I was bored with him. He wasn't very affectionate nor did he compliment me a lot. Thus, I didn't realize how starved I was for attention until I got to this little lust-filled island and I was the "star of the show".

Orlando and I had a good time and we kept each other laughing. He told me he didn't have a girlfriend and I lied and said I was separated. We left the casino and went for a walk and he suggested that we walk through a park. I resisted and he threw words I'd recently said to him back in my face. "You said that you like when a man takes control and now I'm taking control. Walk with me through this park." Like a little girl, I did as I was told and couldn't believe it.

While in the park, he pulled me to him and kissed me on the lips. My lips quivered and I got scared and pushed him back. He held me tighter and kissed me again and forced his tongue in my mouth. To my horror, I responded and kissed him back. Immediately afterward, the realization of what I'd just done, rushed in on me! I couldn't believe the little "DT" was doing a little more than teasing! How could I do this to my husband? What the hell was my problem? I began to cry!

Orlando hugged me and asked what was wrong. I told him the truth and said I wasn't separated and felt guilty that I'd let this go so far. I apologized to him and told him I just wanted to go back to the room. Instead, he talked to me and told me I didn't need to feel guilty because we hadn't done anything.

We talked for a couple more hours and then he walked me back to the hotel. It was like I had transformed into another woman and I didn't like her. I didn't know where she'd come from. I thought that "fast girl" was dead and gone and I couldn't believe that she was back with a vengeance as a full grown woman instead of a pre-adolescent girl. Orlando brought out a side of me I hadn't seen in years and a part of me liked being uninhibited and not the "goody-two-shoes" I'd become. I guess he wasn't so "safe" after all.

When I left with him, I considered him a safe little boy that I could control. I wouldn't have gone out with a man I was terribly attracted to that I felt could manipulate me into "losing my mind". To my complete surprise, he turned out to be a young man who knew how to push my buttons.

We agreed to see each other on his day off the next day. Instead we talked on the phone and weren't able to see one another until the 4th of July, which was my last night on the island. We spent half the day and the entire evening together. When he got off work, he took me to his apartment. I couldn't believe I was there. I didn't feel that he'd rape me but I didn't know what we'd do next since I'd already done something I didn't think I was capable of and kissed him.

He broke out the soft music & champagne and we intertwined our arms and sipped from long stemmed glasses while looking into one another's eyes. It was very romantic. He wanted to take it further but I knew I couldn't allow that. Hell, I had remained a virgin till marriage but here I was about to commit adultery! This didn't add up to the Robin I'd come to love and respect.

I pushed him away and told him that I wanted to go to one of the tourist attractions he'd promised to take me to. He said it was still too early and that we'd have to wait until after sundown. I said I didn't feel comfortable in his apartment and wanted to leave. He convinced me to stay and promised he'd leave me alone because he didn't want to see me cry again.

He took a shower and when he came out, I was curled up in a fetal position drifting off to sleep. He laid down next to me, hugged me and went to sleep also. We woke up right after sundown and left.

We had a good time at the tourist hot spot. We ate ice cream and talked while we waited for the club to get jumping. Once in there, we danced, laughed and acted like we were the only ones in the world that mattered. After we left, he took me to a restaurant for dinner and we hung out there for a while. It began to thunder and rain from out of nowhere and neither of us was dressed for it. So we took shelter in the restaurant and talked.

I found him to be interesting and good natured. He reminded me a lot of Ced and how I felt about him when I first met him. He was sweet and gentle. He didn't push and make me do something I didn't want to do – I realized that he could have raped me while I slept on his bed – but he didn't. Ced was the same way. We would entice each other to a point but then my conscience would kick in and we'd have to stop.

Orlando told me that he wished we'd met each other before I got married so that we could be together. He stated he'd never felt this way about any other woman and really liked the sensations it gave him. I responded that I suspected he and most of the other Jamaican men just preyed on American women until they got one to marry them. He tried to reassure me that he wasn't that way and that I was the only American he'd gotten this close to. I don't think I fully believed him but I wanted to. Then again, I realized that most of the men who got most of the action from Americans were the bartenders - not the ones in Housekeeping. LOL!

When the rain finally ceased, we went for another long walk because we didn't want the evening to end. It was amazing how much stuff we had to talk about. We stayed together until just before dawn. When it was time to separate, we both cried and it took at least three attempts before we could successfully pull away from each other's embrace. He gave me his number and address and I gave him my cell and work address. We promised to keep in touch, if to be nothing more than friends.

When I boarded a plane back to America a few hours later, Orlando was all I could think about. I replayed all of the events. I was flabbergasted that I could kiss and spend so much time with a man I hardly knew while being married. I was absolutely repulsed by my actions. Yes Ced was boring and getting on my nerves but he didn't deserve infidelity. I had to figure out what my problem was, nip it in the bud and move on so that I didn't do this crap again. I felt safe knowing that Orlando was in Jamaica and "what happens in Jamaica stays in Jamaica."

When I finally arrived home, I told my husband that I committed adultery. He told me it was okay and that he still loved me. I said, "What? Did you hear what I just said? I said I committed adultery and you're saying it's okay?"

He calmly replied, "Yes because I know you didn't."

"Well not literally but Jesus said if you lustfully think about someone other than your spouse, you've committed adultery in your heart and I've done this."

"Yes, but it's not the same as doing it. We can get past this and I love you. I suffer from lust too."
I couldn't believe him. He was truly a remarkable man and I was determined not to break his heart. I couldn't figure out the root-cause of why I was so vulnerable. However, I stated that not receiving enough attention from him, and feeling bad about my weight, did play a part in making me an easy target for another man who showered me with compliments.

I apologized to him and he apologized to me for not making me feel special.

God, I loved my husband, but I knew I wasn't done yet. I had to break this stronghold Orlando had on me. He sent me a postcard of a boat drifting in the water and told me that he wished the two of us could get in that boat and drift off to paradise. He also said he loved me and hoped we could marry one day. Was this a fantasy or what?

We talked off and on from July till December, 2004. Most times he called me and with each call I tried to distance myself from him because I felt so guilty. I was relieved when the calls ceased and I was able to completely focus on my relationship with God and my husband. I was relieved that both of them had forgiven me for my indiscretion.

****

On a side note: I'd like to state that some may think it's unwise to divulge so much and let you know that I was tempted again. However, there are others who think that God's people need to become more "real" and talk about their struggles. *Praying doesn't immediately change our behavior. It is a process.* So after much prayer, I've decided to share the process I went through on my way to healing. Perhaps you'll be less likely to judge harshly but rather gain a better understanding, if not empathize.

Have you ever been surprised by a skeleton bone falling out of your closet when you least expected it to? You may have even thought you buried all the bones and gotten rid of all traces of their existence. Well, a bone showed up big as day in February, 2007.

While at work, Orlando called me on my work phone and cell and shocked the living hell out of me! I was so caught off guard by his call that I didn't even recognize his voice. I really didn't expect to hear from him ever again and was relieved that he was a thing of the past. I soon recovered from the shock of hearing from him and felt safe knowing that he was way in Jamaica and we couldn't recapture the past and act on our emotions.

Imagine the "heart attack" I had when he told me that he now lived 90 minutes from me! I almost fell outta my chair! He told me that he married a woman who reminded him of me and was able to move to the States. I never dreamed that he would be in my own backyard but apparently he did because he dropped one more bombshell on me.

"I told you that I would see you again and that one day I'd show up knocking on your door. Well, here I am and I'm knocking. I've missed you and think about you often."

He had only been in the States and married for four months before he contacted me. "I told my wife all about you and explained that you were a good friend I wanted to see again and she thought it would be a good idea for the two of us to have lunch to catch up on old times."

I really couldn't believe those last words. After talking for three weeks, I agreed to meet him for lunch. I tried to reason that nothing would happen and we could rekindle a "platonic relationship".

There's a reason that **Jeremiah 17:9** says: *"The heart is more treacherous than anything else and is desperate. Who can know it?"* and **Proverbs 28:26** says: *"He that is trusting in his own heart is stupid."*

I fell for the "okey doke", as my mama would say, and we went miniature golfing together. We had a good time but he made it very clear that he wanted more than a platonic friendship.

He hadn't seen me in almost three years and I had changed a lot. I lost over 100 pounds and looked completely different from what he remembered. His mouth fell open and he couldn't stop staring at me. The "Coca-Cola" figure was back and it wasn't oversized.

He uttered, "I've always thought you were beautiful and sexy. I still have your pictures and didn't think it was possible for you to be more appealing to me. I was wrong. You are absolutely gorgeous. I can't believe it!"

I was pleased at his reaction. A part of me took a chance on seeing him again so that he could see the "new and improved Robin". Resisting the temptation to kiss each other was too much for us to bear and we were back to where we were in 2004. So much for: "What happens in Jamaica stays in Jamaica."

He told me that his dream was being fulfilled and he hoped that we could continue seeing each other.

"I never forgot about you and getting married didn't take you off my mind. You see that I contacted you almost as soon as I got here. I have to have you in my life and I KNOW that God brought us together or else we wouldn't be sitting here right now. What are the chances of this happening by mistake? It was meant to be. Don't you agree?"

No, I didn't agree though it would be nice to think that were true. Satan also has a way of bringing two people together that shouldn't be.

We met on a Friday and over that weekend I wrote in my "Prayer Journal" and asked Jesus to forgive me. I couldn't continue this and begged Him to help me to stop. I talked to Orlando on that following Tuesday. He told me that he was going to go back to Jamaica for three months and intended to continue talking to me while he was over there. I told him that we couldn't continue this and he asked why. That was such a stupid question. Wasn't the answer obvious?

"Don't you know that this is wrong? We're both married and God will punish us for this - not to mention how our spouses would feel."

"Well I don't really think it's wrong because I love you and I think you love me too, whether you want to admit it or not. It's just too bad that you married him when you did. If you hadn't, we would be married because I never would have married her if you would have left him. Until we decide to leave our spouses, we'll just have to see each other as often as we can. I'm NOT letting you go."

I couldn't believe what I was hearing but I did like his desire for me. Here comes the competition. He was a newlywed and should be in marital bliss but all he could think about was me! This thought really boosted my ego, yet I had to try to convince him to let me go so it would be easier for me to resist this lustful "paradise" we'd created.

A Rude Awakening

"Look, don't you feel guilty? You just got married."

"Well, at church on Sunday, the pastor talked about the Ten Commandments and how we shouldn't covet the wife of another man. I thought about it and realized that's exactly what I'm doing but I can't help it. You should be my wife anyway."

He wasn't easily deterred and I was trying not to weaken my resolve to cut this off and replied, "Well then if it's in the Bible, you know it's a sin. God didn't bring us together and we have to cut this off now. I can't hurt Jehovah, Jesus and The Holy Spirit this way. Please don't call me anymore. I can't take it."

He was understandably ticked and agreed to leave me alone but ended our conversation with, "You know you can't stay away from me. I'll let you have your little time, but we'll talk again because it's meant to be."

The other part of **Proverbs 28:26** says: *"He that is walking in wisdom is the one that will escape."* I hoped throwing myself on the mercy of God and trying to do things HIS way would help me to escape from this trap that was obviously set by Satan. Satan or not, I knew my flesh was weak and that it played a part in this lapse in judgment.

True to Orlando's word, he tried to come back and I was trying to deny my flesh and think about what meant the most to me – my relationship with God and my husband.

Trying not to talk to him was so hard. It's like when you go on a diet and try hard to stay away from chocolate cake and ice cream. You can go two months. However, once you give into your desires to have one bite, one bite isn't enough and before you know it, you've devoured those sinful treats and gone on a three-day binge.

I tearfully reiterated my request for him to stop calling me and to leave me alone. I told him that I had too much to lose and emphasized that I was trying to be a good Christian wife and daughter of

God and I couldn't do that if we continued to communicate.

He finally acquiesced and said, "I love you enough to realize that I have to let you go. I don't like seeing you like this. I'm not as close with God as you are. I don't even think I'm saved. I go to church most Sundays but I'm not even baptized. I don't feel guilty like you do because I think we're meant to be together and I believe God understands. However, you feel differently. So if God is telling you to leave me, then I can't fight with Him. I would be foolish to try. I love you enough to let you go but I'll miss you because I really love you. Can we at least be friends? We can introduce each other to our spouses and then we all can be friends. I just don't want to lose you forever. You mean too much to me. So if I can't be your lover or husband, I'll settle for being your friend."

Those words shocked me. They made me believe that he really loved me and would do anything just to have me apart of his life. He told me that the four of us being friends would probably keep us from committing adultery. I wished that were true but I wasn't convinced.

169

It was during this time that I began writing in my "Prayer Journal" about how I could have gotten to this point. I saw the movie I talked about earlier, and remembered how the abuse began. As I wrote, I began to reopen my wounds and hoped I could clean them out and let them heal properly. For the first time I realized that my fling with Orlando didn't just happen. It started years before I met him and was going to take awhile before I could totally free myself from this stronghold. It was mind-boggling to comprehend that something that happened over two decades before, was the root cause of my vulnerability problem now.

Before leaving for Kenya, I told Ced about Orlando. I told him that I kissed him and that I was devastated by my actions.

"I know a part of the reason I was so vulnerable was because you don't show me the affection I beg you for and you don't compliment me. I really need that so when he came along offering me that, I couldn't resist. Please know that this doesn't excuse my actions but does explain them. Then on top of that, remembering my abuse has helped me to discover that I like illicit attention. Having secret attention is what I got as a child and as twisted as it seems, I'm drawn to that. Know that I'm not telling you this to hurt or blame you but to heal. I need to be honest with you so that I can get better and I don't actually have sex with him or anyone else for that matter."

Once again, my husband rose to the occasion. "I accept my share of responsibility for what has happened. I'm sorry that I've been ignoring you because I do love you very much. I know how hard it is to fight lust. My ex-girlfriend, whom I see from time to time when I visit her mom, came onto me and wanted to have sex the other day. I resisted her and told her that I loved you too much and couldn't do this. I left and I don't plan to ever talk to her or her mom again because I might not be as strong next time."

We hugged, kissed and made love. The next day, I took off work and we went on a date to the movies and had lunch. I really love my husband. Though we obviously have our issues as ALL couples do, our relationship wasn't in shambles and we could make this work. I was glad I confided in him because we drew closer. He finally got "a clue" and began showing me affection. I just wanted it to last.

God forgave me again and I went to Kenya. While there, I was in my room praising and worshipping in a way I had never done before. During that time, The Holy Spirit told me that He wasn't going to punish me for what I'd done with Orlando and had totally forgiven me. I couldn't believe it because I was thinking of ways He should punish me because I totally deserved it! He showed me mercy instead and used me to perform miracles. He even used me to heal a crippled young man and I witnessed him walk! The whole hospital ward broke out in applause for our Maker!

I was on fire for God and determined not to break His heart again and "take His kindness for weakness".

When I came back from Kenya, I saw that Orlando had sent me two e-mails. One invited Ced and me to his home for a party and the other asked me to call him. I didn't respond to either. Later he sent me an e-mail asking me if I was mad at him. Again, I didn't respond. It felt good to ignore him and I was determined to move forward and not get sucked back into a relationship with him. I had too much to lose.

Over the next year, Orlando would send me e-mail forwards, text messages and left voicemails. Though I liked knowing that I was still on his mind, I felt stronger with each passing day that I didn't respond.

One time he left a message saying, "Do you really want to spend the rest of your life with him when it's obvious you really want me and you're staying with him because you think it's the right thing to do? If you're concerned about Raven, I know I've never met her, but she'll eventually love having me as her stepfather. I promise you that we'll both be happy if we divorce our spouses and get married. You may think I'm being selfish but you have to think of yourself first or who else will? Think about it and call me."

His words reminded me of my mama's. She always said, "Self-preservation is the first law of nature."

Yeah and self-preservation led to me being molested and having to watch her marry that animal and have more children with him. I'm sure she didn't think she was putting her "man" before me, but that's exactly what she did. I REFUSED to put Raven through that.

I didn't want my child to suffer from sexual abuse and I KNEW that Ced would NEVER harm her but I wasn't so sure about Orlando. He would become her stepfather and although I know the majority of stepfathers do not abuse, a strong minority of them do. I couldn't put my child in harm's way. Don't get me wrong. Orlando didn't do anything that would make me think he was a molester but then again, it's the ones we trust that hurt us the most. Ced had proven he was trustworthy and I would rather bet on him keeping our daughter safe over anyone else. I would NEVER forgive myself if Raven was molested because of my selfishness.

This went on for a year and finally he burned himself out and I haven't heard from him in over a year! What really helped in my deliverance from these symptoms of **Taboo** (the twisted desire for illicit attention and a competitive, self-destructive spirit) was when my husband prayed over me.

Cedric got on his knees and **prayed that the stronghold be broken.** He asked Orlando's name and then used his name in the prayer. I lifted my arms towards the ceiling and cried as I pulled my wrists apart; it felt like shackles were being broken off me. For the FIRST time since this ordeal began in 2004 - five whole years before - I felt healed. **The chains of sexual bondage were broken! HALLELUJAH & THANK YOU JESUS!!!**

Another tool that has assisted in my healing is writing this book. It has helped me to be honest with myself so that I can not only get healing for me, but others too. Being honest hasn't been easy. I've done it at the risk of being perceived as an ungodly woman. Yet, I know that isn't true. *I was wounded and weak but not wicked and heartless.*

In John 8, a woman who was caught in adultery was brought to Jesus so that she could be stoned. They thought Jesus would throw the first stone. Did He?

In part, **John 8:7, 10, 11** says: *"He that is without sin, cast the first stone....woman, did they not condemn you? Neither do I condemn you."*

May those words also comfort you if you can relate to what I've shared and may feel that the sins you committed may be too big to be forgiven - especially if you feel that you can't forgive yourself. As I said before, to deal with the pain of **Taboo**, we have acted in ways that may cause us shame. You still can recover. ***With God's help, I did and so can you.***

During this time, I realized something. I couldn't help but notice that before every ministerial milestone, the devil tempted me with Orlando. Don't get me wrong, my flesh played its part too. I don't believe in: "the devil made me do it!" However, I am not naïve and can see the devil's hand in all of this. Orlando believed it was God's Hand at work but I knew better.

Going through this has also given Ced and me a new appreciation for one another. We have come through the roughest patch in our marriage. I don't know what the devil has up the road but

I DO KNOW that Jehovah, Christ Jesus & the Holy Spirit have prepared us for it. Not only are we prepared for the temptations and tribulations, but we're prepared for the spiritual/physical blessings and prosperity that are up the road too because we weathered the storm. *Glory to GOD!*

Chapter 14 ~ A Family's Shame Becoming Gain
Taboo Stories of Other Family Members

As I told you at the beginning of this book, **Taboo** is about incest or molestation that has occurred in my family. Unfortunately, it wasn't limited to me. It began long before I was born.

Taboo has occurred on both sides of my family. I have at least three cousins on my mother's side who were habitually molested by various people – in and outside of the family. I have at least two aunts and two cousins who were molested on my father's side of the family. One was my male cousin, Tamar, who was molested by a male mortician as a child. Tragically, this eventually led to him committing suicide, two months before my father did, while he was finishing up his last year of college. On a side note: There have been three suicides in our family – all of them males. My father's younger brother, Garland, my cousin, Tamar and my father.

Now take a journey with two of my paternal relatives, Bettye & Crystal, as they reveal their **Taboo** secrets.

****
Bettye

My Aunt Bettye is a beautiful, accomplished woman. She was quite precocious at an early age. The fact that she was reading the Bible at the tender age of six attests to that. She was also full of spunk and that trait was noticed by predators. This is her story.

A few years ago, I was watching a movie about incest and I couldn't believe how hard I was crying! Sometimes things are buried so deep that you forget all about them, but this movie dredged up memories of me being about four or five when my daddy's brother began molesting me. He was so depraved that he commented that even when I was a baby, I had a fat vagina. How sick is that? Even while I was an infant, he was checking me out!

He would often smile at me and see how close he could get to me without anyone noticing. He would put me on his lap and then grind his penis against my butt. This would happen in his house. After he saw that he could get away with that, he progressed to more acts of depravity. He would then take his penis out and have me to massage it while he fingered my vagina. To keep me cooperative, he would give me candy or money.

Unfortunately, this wasn't the only family member who got his "rocks off" on me. One of my maternal aunt's husbands messed with me too. He started off putting me on his lap around the same time as my other perverted uncle. He lived down the street from us and would entice me to his house when my aunt was away. He'd pull out his penis and have me touch him while he manipulated my clit. He had to give me money and candy too.

The bastard also molested his daughters and granddaughters. He was a minister and even got a thirteen-year-old girl in his church pregnant! He was excommunicated but that didn't stop him from preying on young girls – **girls he should have prayed for and NOT preyed on.**

My story is a little different because I "flipped the script", so to speak. Instead of them threatening me and my family if I told, I threatened to tell on them if they didn't give me the money that I sweetly asked for. From that time onward, I learned how to use men. I like to say that their "hardness is their weakness". In other words, a hard penis makes a soft mind. They thought they could get me? Please, I got them back and loved the power my sexuality gave me.

It seemed like men didn't have self-control when they were around me. Several preachers attempted to seduce me when I was a teenager. That really disgusted me since they professed to be "men of God". Oftentimes when I would baby-sit for people, the husbands would try to get me to sleep with them while they were taking me home. They were so weak and it sickened me. I was beginning to not have much use for men unless it was to get something I wanted.

In my early twenties, I decided that men were boring and predictable, with sex utmost on their little minds. I'm sure this led me to explore relationships with women. I found them to be more sensuous and more fun. For almost ten years I was bi-sexual and had loving, exciting relationships with women because I felt that women were more deserving of me than men.

It seemed like even "straight" women were turned on by me. I had a hairdresser who braided my hair in her home. One night, she rubbed up against me while braiding my hair and it escalated into sex. This happened twice. Looking back, I wondered what made her think I was attracted to women. I wasn't what people would call a "butch". On the contrary, I'm very feminine. However, I do remember that I complimented her on her little waist and big butt - maybe that's what let her know it was okay.

In retrospect, I believe that my fascination with women probably came as a result of my disdain for men. Once I dealt with that, I no longer felt a "need" for women and decided that I wanted to have another child. I had a son (my second child in twenty years) and eventually married four more times.

****

Aunt Bettye is a very talented woman who became very successful. She has traveled around the world with several well-known artists as a back-up singer, was in several movies, became a high school teacher, started a Charter high school and authored four books.

In fact, her latest book, *From Survivor to Thriver* began as a journal of what she went through in the aftermath of her eighteen-year-old son's murder. Many months later, she realized that she should turn it into a "self-help" book and help other suffering mothers. She then developed a *Write to Heal* program for secondary school youth and parents who suffer from PTSD (Post-Traumatic Stress Disorder) and a PTSD Sensitivity Training for teachers to empower them to teach this population.

Her motto: *"When life gives you lemons, make lemon meringue pie!"* Like my aunt, you can do the same. Don't just stop at making lemonade, make pie!

As you can see, like many women – maybe even you – my aunt used men's weaknesses against them so that she couldn't be hurt again. That even led to her developing lesbian relationships. It's not uncommon. In fact, it's very common. I would venture to say that most women, who experience lesbian relationships, do so as a reaction to being victimized or abused by men. Is this the best way to deal with the abuse? No it isn't and I pray that God helps you to heal completely so that you're able to have a relationship that truly honors Him.

****

Crystal

Crystal is my favorite female cousin on my dad's side and is Bettye's beautiful daughter from her first husband. She was between nine and ten when her abuse occurred.

I lived with my maternal grandparents. My grandfather was a preacher and my grandmother was a missionary. We often had people stay in our home who were passing through town. A preacher and friend of the family in his forties or fifties needed to stay with us for a few days. I slept in the living room and gave up my room to him so he could be more comfortable.

In the middle of the night, I was awakened by him leaning over me and telling me to be quiet. He then pulled down my blanket, pulled up my gown and pulled down my panties. He began doing oral sex on me and once he was satisfied, marched back into my room as if nothing had happened!

I was in shock and cried. I didn't understand what had just happened to me. Unlike today, over thirty years ago, they didn't show this kind of thing on TV or even allude to it. Hell, they didn't even show bra commercials without the bra being on the outside of a fully clothed woman. They didn't allow you to see skin. In some sitcoms, they didn't even show the husband and wife sleeping in the same bed.

So I really didn't know what had just happened. I was mortified and confused. However, the next morning, I told my grandparents. I don't remember what they said to console me, but I do remember hearing them yell at him. I was told to go to school. I later called my daddy. He was furious and when he picked me up from school, he had a gun and we went looking for that preachin' jackass. Of course, he was nowhere to be found and we never saw him again.

I felt safe and protected when my father came to my rescue. I really needed that because the subject was never brought up again by my grandparents. It was as if nothing ever happened. Years later, I mentioned it to my grandmother and she didn't even remember the incident. In those days, they didn't know how to deal with child molestation. It was just "hushed up and swept under the rug". Thankfully, we know more today and I hope this book helps you to break the cycle in either your life or others.

I didn't even remember the incident until I was in my twenties in a drug rehab and saw a movie in which a little boy was being molested. It all came back. I broke down and cried until I had no more tears. I was so devastated that I couldn't finish the rehab and left a couple days later. I needed a "fix" and heroin would do the trick or so I thought.

Strangely enough, that incident didn't make me more curious about sex. However, I did begin smoking weed at thirteen. Did the molestation lead to this? I don't think it did. I had other stuff going on in my life. I adored my grandfather and he suffered a stroke when I was about that age and then died three years later. I chose to lose myself in drugs and a boyfriend that could always get them for me.

I became a mother at sixteen and had a total of four boys with this loser.

I later lost my boys and they went to stay with their dad's abusive grandmother and grandfather. Sadly, my kids really suffered while their mother used heroin and their dad was in and out of jail.

Unlike many drug addicts, I was never homeless nor did I need to steal. I used men to get me what I needed and they readily complied. Some were white, some were rich but all were sprung on me. They got what they needed from me and I got what I needed from them. As my aunt Sheila, Robin's mom would say, "Fair exchange ain't no robbery."

Later, the prayers of my grandmother and other family members prevailed because I got cleaned up. I've been sober for close to twenty years and I'm happy to say that I'm married to a wonderful man and there is true, mutual love between us.

I have tried to restore my relationship with my boys and I am a proud grandmother of eight. I never thought I could hold down a job because I never had to, but I run our company's medical billing department and own my own home. I must say that I'm proud of what I've accomplished. Like my mom, I took the lemons life gave me and made lemon meringue pie!

****

Yes, abuse has had a terrible stranglehold on some in our family but thankfully, it doesn't define us. Did you notice that all of our memories of **Taboo** were triggered by a movie? That astounded me! It is amazing how movies, books, etc. can serve to help us start the healing process. Addressing the past, learning from it and not merely "glossing over" it, leads to lasting, triumphant healing and victorious accomplishments!

I'm sure you can attest to the accomplishments you've made despite the abuse. Guess what? There's more success up the road. Just be determined not to let old "tapes" play in your head and act destructively as a result.

You are better than the pervert that hurt you. May the added strength you gain from hearing about others with stories similar to yours, move you to your next triumph!

Chapter 15 ~ Breaking the Generational Curse

As I mentioned in Chapter 4, sexual abuse can become a curse that is passed down from one generation to the next (as in our family). Before I go into tools that you can use to combat this issue, let me clear up what I mean by "generational curse". I don't mean that some witch placed a curse on our family and said that many girls will be molested. While that's not the case, I do believe that "curses" can be manifested through certain sins, problems or sicknesses and diseases that can be passed down from one generation to the next.

I'm not saying that every problem in your life is the result of your forefathers' sins and thereby a curse. To help you better understand when something could be a generational curse or not, consider this: Let's say that you have breast cancer, and so did your mom, grandmother and a couple aunts. This could indicate that a curse is manifesting itself and needs to be broken. However, if only you and your grandmother had it, perhaps it's not and just an opportunity God can use to get glory and heal you. Believe it or not, it's scriptural.

In part, **Exodus 34:7** says: *"Jehovah pardons error and sins but by no means will He give exemption from punishment, bringing punishment for the error of fathers upon sons and upon grandsons, upon the third generation and upon the fourth generation."*

Now this doesn't mean that you're forever doomed by things that happened in your family. Jesus' blood is strong enough to wash us from that but we have to acknowledge the sins of our forefathers and ask forgiveness and clemency from it. This doesn't mean that we need to know each and every sin and call it out by name. We can simply ask the Lord, who knows what particular sins are oppressing us, to wash us clean and relieve us of their consequences and break the cycle. Otherwise, the devil can say that he has legal grounds to punish us from past generational sins based upon the above principle.

Of course, my forefathers didn't knowingly set me or my other family members up to be molested. Yet, when we disregard Godly principles, it can reap a harvest that we never thought possible. It can be manifested through various things, such as suicide, molestation, alcoholism, sickness and disease. Today's world doesn't put much "stock" in what the Bible says, but that doesn't make the curses and even blessings that come from either adhering or not adhering to it, any less potent.

Deuteronomy 30:19 says: *"I do take the heavens and the earth as witnesses against you that I have put life and death before you, the blessing and the malediction (curse); and you must choose life....by loving Jehovah and listening to His voice and sticking to Him."*

The above verse mentions blessings. We can also declare and decree blessings upon us that began in earlier generations. Just as curses can be passed down, so can the blessings as is brought out at **Deuteronomy 7:9**. It says that God will bless or show *"loving-kindness in the case of those loving Him and those who keep his commandments down to the thousandth generation."*

I know the foregoing was pretty deep and perhaps you've never heard anything like it before. You may even disagree. That's fine. We don't have to agree on everything. However, it is what I believe and for those who have similar beliefs, I think I would be doing this book disservice, if I didn't discuss the spiritual affect of **Taboo** and what we can do to combat it and the devil that is ultimately responsible for it. So please bear with me as I proceed.

As you can see with both sides of my family, at least two generations were affected by **Taboo**. How can it be stopped? How can you keep your daughter, son or other family members from falling prey to this depravity?

Prayer and vigilance. What? Does that sound too simple or weird? Perhaps it does. This is especially so if you're not a Christian and don't completely understand the **Power of Prayer**. It may sound like a lame way to combat or attack a problem. However, Jesus said in **Matthew 17:20**: "If you *have faith the size of a mustard seed, you will tell a mountain to transfer from here to there and it will transfer. Nothing will be impossible for you.*" He also said in **John 14:14**: "If you *ask anything in my name I will do it.*"

You may be wondering how you can put this principle into action. Oftentimes, things in the Bible were symbols of things in heaven. For example, a dove and olive/anointing oil were symbols of God's Holy Spirit and a request for God's favor. I began to break the curse over my daughter (and by extension, others in the next generation) by anointing Raven with olive oil that I had prayed over. I then commanded the devil to keep his filthy, depraved hands off of my daughter. I also begged Jesus to allow His protective, sacrificial blood to cover her and not allow anyone to molest, kidnap or in any way harm her.

I know this sounds very strange. Before I realized **the power God has given us over evil,** I thought so too. However, now I know differently because I see Him answer prayers continually. I've even seen Him use me to heal people. Therefore, I know that it is an easy thing for Him to keep my baby safe from predators. I also know that He is no respecter of persons and what He does for me He can do for you too.

Life and death are in the tongue. In fact, everything God wanted to be created, He "spoke or decreed it" first. Read Genesis chapters 1 and 2. With every creation He said: "Let there be...and it came to be."

We can do the same thing. We can choose to speak or decree life to a situation and have faith that if it's according to God's will, it will come to pass. Or we can speak death to a situation by being negative and that may come to pass also.

For example, if I said that being molested was just a part of my family and it will never change. Guess what? It probably wouldn't. On the other hand, if I get tough with this curse or depravity and say that "the buck stops with me" and that I refuse to let my daughter fall victim to this, she won't.

The other tool is recognizing our sins and those of our forefathers, as I mentioned earlier. We can beg God to forgive us for everything that we've done that would make the devil feel like he has "license or authority" over us and ask God to cover us with Jesus' life-saving blood. We then can rest in the comfort of knowing that He longs to respond to heart-felt prayers for His forgiveness, direction and love.

Reading scriptures and speaking God's Word back to Him is very powerful too. He can't lie and He has to honor His Word. The following scriptures are my favorite and back up the fact that God wants to be there for us when we need Him. So when I'm going through distressing times, I remind our Father of His Word and I have faith that He will respond accordingly. Granted, it doesn't always happen as quickly as I'd like, but He is always right on time. Perhaps you'd like to add these to your **"spiritual toolbox"** also.

****

Psalm 55:22: *"Throw your burden upon Jehovah and He Himself will sustain you. Never will He allow the righteous one to totter."*

Psalm 145:16: *"He is opening His hand and satisfying the desire of every living thing."*

Romans 8:28: *"Now we know that God makes all His works cooperate for the good of those who love God."*

Connecting prayers with other practical measures is needed too. Therefore, being vigilant and watchful of all who come into contact with your child is imperative. If someone gives you a "creepy" feeling, trust it. If your child expresses discomfort or dislike for a person, listen to them. Children generally have good instincts.

Children love "sleepovers". However, not everyone can be trusted with your child overnight. There are a very limited number of people that I will allow to keep Raven overnight. It may seem overprotective, but "better safe than sorry".

What will you do? You have been given some basic tools in breaking the generational curse on your family, (if there is one), and not allowing one to start, (if there isn't). If you need assistance, ask a trusted minister to help you to do this. Even if you feel weird doing so, what do you really have to lose? Nothing, but you have everything to gain. Go ahead and approach God's Throne. **He's waiting for you.** (smile!)

Chapter 16 ~ The Revelation: Walking in Victory

We've finally come to the end of the book. I know that at times it may have been a painful journey but you kept walking with me. We've discussed how **Taboo** can birth a self-destructive and competitive spirit within us. We've also discussed the importance of forgiveness – first for yourself and then for your abuser. You were reminded how it is imperative that you heal and prosper despite the horror you experienced.

What will you do with this information or better yet, what have you already done with it? Have you begun to understand yourself a little better and why you behave and react to things the way you do? Are you more aware of why you made certain decisions that you may have not made had you not been molested?

Do you feel better about yourself and more determined than ever to "turn the lemons you were given into lemon meringue pie"? You are so very precious and as you've learned, it's easy to forget that fact and cheat yourself out of achieving the ultimate, complete, successful picture of you.

Why do I say picture? When we look back on our lives, we tend to focus on memories or "pictures" of our past. We can get stuck on the blemish on the picture and not the whole image. Yes, you were wounded but that's a small blemish compared to the dynamic person you are. No doubt you've already accomplished things that you minimize because you don't value it as much as those who admire you. Why not embrace your victories more than you embrace the tragedies you've endured?

You are more than a conqueror because you survived one of the best shots the devil could aim your way, and you've continued to persevere. I'm proud of you. Be proud of yourself and continue pushing forward to achieve the ultimate, complete, successful picture of you.

As I stated earlier, I don't know how many steps it's going to take for you to get there, but as long as you keep moving forward, you're going in the right direction.

One important step is to **include Jehovah, Jesus & The Holy Spirit on your journey**. They long to be the center of your life rather than spectators. Won't you let them in?   Remember you are so precious that Jesus laid down His life to usher you into everlasting blessings beyond the pain or curses you've experienced. He would have done it had you been the only person on earth. How does that profound knowledge make you feel? Does it make you want to "pick up the phone and call God"? He's waiting to pick up and devote His attention to you. Why? **He misses and LOVES you more than you or any other human can love you.**

What does the future have in store for you? Are you excited to enter the next chapter of your life? You will *"Walk in Victory"* because you are a fighter and you refuse to just lie down and die. You're too strong for that!   Through this book, you were reminded just how much strength you actually have and how much you have to offer others.

Perhaps you know someone else who has been molested. Encourage them to get a copy of **Taboo** and tell them to take this journey of self discovery and ultimate victory over a tragedy that was meant to tear them to shreds. May you be there for them when they need a shoulder to cry on and remind them that they are not alone and it **WAS NOT THEIR FAULT.**

Thank you for allowing me to share **Taboo** with you and I pray that the book has blessed you as God and I intended. Feel free to visit my website *(www. comeoninwithrobin. com)* and e-mail me when you need to talk. **We can be there for each other.**

Please allow me to close in prayer.

> *Dearest Father, I thank You for empowering me to write **Taboo**. The devil wanted the tragedy I experienced to keep me bound in a self-destructive cycle. Yet you said differently. You had me to get to know not only me, but You better through this and I now experience joy versus sorrow. I thank You for using **Taboo** to minister to the needs of others who have a similar story. May they realize that You want to be apart of this journey with them and usher them into a victorious future beyond their imagination. If they don't know You, I pray that they will*

have the courage to say a prayer similar to the following:

Jesus, thank You for leaving Your comfortable home in heaven to take on flesh and experience this world that can cause so much pain. Thank You for dying on Calvary to buy me back from the gates of hell in order to usher me into Your pearly gates of heaven. I know that You were born of a virgin, died and was raised on the third day. Therefore, I repent of my sins and beg You to forgive me and enable me to forgive others. Please cleanse me of my sins and any curses that may be attached to them that could affect me or my family. I love You and want You to take over and become my Lord & Savior forever. In Jesus' Name I pray, Amen.

*Father, now that they've prayed this prayer with a sincere heart, please give them peace to know that they are now saved and have no choice but to **walk in victory**. In Jesus' Name, Amen.*

Welcome into the family of God! The best is yet to come because **Taboo** is now a thing of the past as you run towards your victorious future!

ABOUT THE AUTHOR

Robin Sweet-Ransom is the proud wife of Cedric Ransom and doting mother of Raven Ransom. She is dedicated to fulfilling God's call on her life to reach out to those who are hungering for spiritual and personal growth. This passion has led her to engage in several ventures.

The latest venture was writing **Taboo**. It is her first published book and she hopes that others that have suffered come away feeling that their wounds can finally mend.

Robin also hosted and produced a cable talk show, *"Come On In w/Robin Sweet-Ransom"*, for several years. It is now accessible on internet radio. The show's purpose is to interview guests on topics ranging from domestic abuse to politics. She endeavors to give a fresh perspective which centers upon Godly morals and personal responsibility.

She also has a love for Kenya and fulfilled a lifelong desire to travel to this beautiful country. She spent a lot of time getting to know the needs and aspirations of many people from the cities to the villages. Robin ascertained that they needed 300 Bibles & mentors. She zealously accomplished the goal of fulfilling both needs.

Always *looking forward* to the future with hope, propels Robin forward to embrace the next adventure life has in store for her!